Cross Vision Study Guide

Cross Vision Study Guide

Gregory A. Boyd and Deacon Godsey

Fortress Press
Minneapolis

CROSS VISION STUDY GUIDE

Cover design: Brad Norr Design

Print ISBN: 978-1-5064-4948-7

eBook ISBN: 978-1-5064-4949-4

The paper used in this publication meets the minimum requirements of American National Standard for Information Sciences — Permanence of Paper for Printed Library Materials, ANSI Z329.48-1984.

Manufactured in the U.S.A.

Contents

PART III. THE TRUE NATURE OF GOD'S JUDGMENT

PART IV. SEEING *SOMETHING ELSE* THROUGH THE LOOKING-GLASS CROSS

Introduction

In the summer of 2017, I (Deacon) was privileged to take a three-month sabbatical from pastoral ministry, the first such break in the nearly twenty years our family has been serving together in the local church. Our time away was the single greatest ministry-related gift we have ever received, not only for how it allowed us to reconnect as a family, but also for the time it allowed for contemplative prayer, deep theological study, and the opportunity to meet with some of the theological mentors who had influenced me over the years, but whom I'd never had the chance to meet in person.

Toward the end of this sabbatical, I had the chance to meet Greg Boyd face-to-face, something I'd hoped to do for many, many years. I wanted to thank him for the life-changing impact his work had on my life, and also share my thoughts—and ask some questions—about his most recent project, *The Crucifixion of the Warrior God: Interpreting the Old Testament's Violent Portraits of God in Light of the Cross* (*CWG*).

In Dallas Willard's *The Divine Conspiracy*, Richard Foster's introduction describes Willard's book as "the book I have been searching for all my life." Like many of my generation, I felt the same way, and like many who've read *CWG*, I can honestly say I feel that way again.

For years I had wrestled with what Greg describes as "the violent portraits of God in the Old Testament (OT)," not knowing what to do with them, either in my own life or in my pastoral ministry. Growing up in a fairly conservative "Bible believing" stream of the Christian faith, I was fully committed to the authority and integrity of Scripture, but I honestly couldn't make sense of how God was both perfectly revealed in the person of Jesus and also somehow responsible for the reprehensible violence I saw throughout the OT. I knew a variety of explanations were out there, but none of them could adequately scratch my intellectual or theological itch. They just didn't seem to add up.

So, to be honest—rightly or wrongly—I pretty much avoided the OT in my preaching and discipleship efforts. I had no trouble picking and choosing various passages to highlight, concepts to extrapolate, narrative pictures to paint, and so on, but for the most part, when it came to the OT, I kept it to broad, general themes and most definitely avoided the texts that—for me—were deeply problematic. I didn't want to preach on something I couldn't make sense of or start a conversation I wasn't adequately prepared to engage in.

In the spring of 2017, however, the long-awaited arrival of *CWG* finally came, and despite its monumental size, I devoured it in a couple weeks. It was so great to have a book that looked these troubling passages squarely in the eye, unflinching, and provided a means of interpreting them in a way that unapologetically pointed to Jesus and—somewhat to my surprise—inspired a deeper sense of love for God than I'd experienced before.

Since I'm wired as a teacher, I immediately began thinking of how to condense the depth and breadth of *CWG* into a workable format for the people of Vintage Church where I serve as lead pastor. Since *CWG* is over 1,400 pages, that seemed like a daunting task, but

I knew Greg was releasing his own "popular" version of this massive book later that summer called *Cross Vision: How the Crucifixion of Jesus Makes Sense of Old Testament Violence* (*CV*), so I was hopeful some of that work had been done for me. As I walked through *Cross Vision*, I was not disappointed; I was further inspired to help make Greg's thoughts available to the people of Vintage Church, and perhaps to other churches as well.

You see, having walked with Jesus for over thirty years, and having worked in full-time Christian ministry for two-thirds of that span, I've seen a theme play out increasingly in my own life—and, sadly, in the discipleship efforts of the church as a whole—that I summarize like this:

> A messed up reading of the Bible
> Leads to messed up beliefs and narratives about God
> Which leads to messed up people
> Saying and doing messed up things (often in the name of God or under the banner of Jesus)
> All of which greatly diminishes our ability to effectively love God with everything we have
> And to love our neighbors as ourselves.

This is largely why this *Cross Vision Study Guide* was created, as it seeks to address, at the root level, the problem of how we read, interpret, and ultimately seek to apply Scripture in our day-to-day lives.

By considering Greg's cruciform hermeneutic,[1] we hope to develop a more life-giving, God-honoring, Spirit-directed reading of Scripture that truly places the revelation of God in Jesus Christ at the center of all biblical interpretation and application, with the hope that as our reading of Scripture becomes more Christ-centered, so will our beliefs about, and worship of, God. As our beliefs and narratives

---

1. Cruciform = reflecting the revelation of God we see in Jesus dying on the cross for his enemies. Hermeneutic = a method of interpretation; in this case: how we go about reading and interpreting the Bible.

about God become more in line with the revelation of God in Christ, so will our lives as a whole; and as we become a more Christlike people, our interactions with one another and the world around us will also become more Christlike.

Using the Study Guide

Cross Vision Study Guide is designed to assist individuals, adult missional communities, small groups, leadership teams, and so on with their personal, church, or organization's discipleship process by

- walking participants through the main points of Greg Boyd's cruciform hermeneutic, as set forth in his book *Cross Vision*,[2] in order to

- help them grasp a more Christ-centered reading of the Bible as a whole, particularly as it relates to the violent portraits of God in the Old Testament, so that

- more Christlike beliefs and narratives about God can emerge, and

- a more Christlike way of interacting with one another and the world can be lived out.

The curriculum includes a suggested ten-week interactive survey of *Cross Vision* (see below), but feel free to adjust that timetable as you see fit. As you walk through each lesson, feel free to allow for dialogue and questions along the way, as each lesson's material is bound to raise a number of questions not specifically listed in this study guide. The more the material is interacted with in community, the better. And of course, it's recommended to open and close each lesson

---

2. See appendix 1 at the end of the study guide for a table summary of the cruciform hermeneutic.

in prayer, asking the Spirit to lead and guide the time of reflection and conversation.

All leaders and participants are encouraged to have a copy of *Cross Vision* and to read the relevant chapter(s) for each week's lesson prior to walking through the study-guide material.

Each lesson (with the exception of the very last one) has the same major components, including:

- **The Big Idea**: summarizing the chapter's main point

- **Finding Jesus**: identifying the chapter's expression of God's self-revelation in Jesus

- **Terms and Definitions**: defining the chapter's major theological concepts

- **References and Reflections**: engaging the chapter's central ideas

  ◦ A summary of Greg's main points from that week's *Cross Vision* chapter

  ◦ A related passage of Scripture with reflection questions

  ◦ Personal study questions to silently engage with the material

  ◦ Questions to process as a group

  ◦ We have left space after each question for readers to write out their thoughts, if they so choose

- **Q&A**: Greg's responses to FAQs he has received on each chapter

- **Recommended Resources**: a brief bibliography of relevant reading on each chapter

(Readers should note that, while Greg was involved in creating and editing all aspects of this study guide, we will refer to him in the third person to preserve a uniform voice, except when Greg is responding to questions and objections.[3])

Regardless of what form your *Cross Vision* experience takes, it is our hope and prayer that each lesson will draw you closer to the beauty of the revelation of God in Jesus, and, "in seeing this . . . [you] will see that the revelation of God on the cross must bring a once-and-for-all end to all of our own violent conceptions of him. . . . For when the sin of the world was nailed to the cross with Christ (Col 2:14), the sinful concept of God as a violent warrior god was included. Hence, the revelation of the *agape*-loving and sin-bearing crucified God entails the permanent crucifixion of the warrior god."[4]

---

3. While Greg believes males and females are equally created in the image of God (Gen 1:26–28), and while he respects those who may disagree with his decision, Greg will in this work follow the convention of referring to God as "he." Among his reasons for following this practice is the fact that he quotes a great deal of Scripture, all of which uses the second person male pronoun to refer to God, and he felt it would be cumbersome as well as distracting to continually adjust his language.

4. Gregory A. Boyd, *Crucifixion of the Warrior God: Interpreting The Old Testament's Violent Portraits of God In Light of The Cross*, 2 vols. (Minneapolis, MN: Fortress, 2017), 1:xli–xlii.

PART I

The Problem and a Looking-Glass Solution

Week #1: Part I—The Elephant: Calling It Like It Is

The old adage about "the elephant in the room" refers to something massive and obvious to anyone paying attention that is totally ignored or denied for one reason or another. It can be as inconsequential as a lingering odor that can't be identified or as meaningful as an important conversation topic everyone knows needs to be addressed but that everyone would much rather avoid. Sometimes the "elephant" is avoided because it seems too awkward and uncomfortable to address, but sometimes it's avoided due to outright fear. It just seems too daunting to tackle.

As Greg points out in *Cross Vision*, the violent portraits of God in Scripture have created just such an "elephant," and it's one we must stop ignoring, avoiding, or dismissing if we're ever going to figure out how such passages actually point us to the revelation of God in the crucified Christ, as we'll later see all Scripture is supposed to do.

THE BIG IDEA: The violent portraits of God in the OT must be faced head on.

FINDING JESUS: "*All* Scripture is inspired by God for the purpose of pointing to him. We just need the ability to see it." (*CV* 16)

TERMS AND DEFINITIONS: Major concepts from this lesson include:

> • **ANE** = ancient Near East; this included nations like Assyria, Canaan, Israel, and many more. The ANE was the context in which all of the OT was written. The reality of this historical context must be faced head on if we are to properly understand the OT, including especially the OT's violent depictions of God

> • *hērem* = to set apart a people group for total destruction as an act of devotion to Yahweh

REFERENCES AND REFLECTIONS:

Here is a summary of Greg's main points from this chapter:

> **The Book Greg Couldn't Write:** "On the authority of Jesus, I had to affirm that the whole OT is divinely inspired. But also on the authority of Jesus, I could no longer accept the violence that some narratives within this divinely inspired book ascribe to God. . . . [I]t was only by acknowledging that the violent portraits of God in the OT were *not* compatible with the God who is fully revealed on the cross that I came to see how these portraits actually *point* to the God who is fully revealed on the cross!" (*CV* 6–7)

Embracing the Problem: "If a biblical author ascribes an action to God that we would normally consider morally awful, [we must] admit that the action is, in fact, morally awful." (*CV* 7)

God Engaging in Violence: "Origen taught that when we come upon a biblical passage that seems unworthy of God, we must humble ourselves before God and ask the Spirit to help us find a deeper meaning in the passage that *is* worthy of God. . . . Like many other Christian thinkers in the first several centuries of church history, Origen considered all the violent portraits of God in the OT to be unworthy of God. Yet these early Christian thinkers didn't feel free to dismiss these portraits, for they firmly believed that *all* Scripture is inspired by God. These thinkers rather believed that *something else was going on* when Scripture represents God in ways that are inconsistent with what is revealed in Christ, and they patiently waited on the Holy Spirit and contemplated what this *something else* might be. As a result, they believed the Spirit helped them discover the Christ-centered, God-glorifying treasure that was buried in the depths of this unworthy material." (*CV* 16)

As you consider Greg's thoughts, please read and reflect on Numbers 31:1–18:

(margin, left side, vertical): JEREMIAH 23:12; 51:56 GOD OF RETRIBUTION | NAHUM 6:2 GOD IS JEALOUS & AVENGING | PUNISHMENT

TO EXECUTE VENGEANCE, WAR
TO CAPTIVE

1. Make a list of the things God seems to command, or at least allow, the Israelites to do in this passage that strike you as incompatible with the revelation of God in the crucified Christ.

VENGEANCE IS MINE SAYS THE LORD
   DEUT 32:35-36 COMPASSION ON HIS SERVANTS
   RBM 12:19
    HEBREWS 10:30 THE LORD WILL JUDGE
    2 Peter 2:3 LONG STANDING VERDICT
    EXODUS 32:34 GREED, I WILL PUNISH
    LEVITICUS 19:18 LOVE NEIGHBOR
    1 SAM 26:10 LORD STRIKE HIM DOWN OR
      PERISH IN BATTLE
    2 KINGS 9:7 STRIKE DOWN THAT I MAY AVENGE
    Jeremiah 8:12 I WILL PUNISH THEM

2. If you had read this passage in another religion's sacred text, what words would you use to honestly express how the passage strikes you? How would you describe the portrait of God in this passage?

WOMEN INTIMATE WITH MAN SLAIN VS 15&16 FOR THEY CAUSED SONS OF ISRAEL THROUGH COUNSEL OF BALAAM to tresspass AGAINST THE LORD

VS 18 - SPARE THE VIRGINS WHY? THEY DID NOT CAUSE MEN OF ISRAEL TO TRESSPASS AGAINST GOD
DOES NOT SAY TO KEEP THEM FOR THE SOLDIERS pleasure
POSSIBLE THE WOMAN WERE KEPT TO BECOME WIFE INTERBREEDING STRENGTHEN SURVIVAL GENETICAL

3. Do you think God actually endorsed Moses giving his men permission to keep captured virgins for their own personal/ sexual pleasure, or that God actually commanded his people to kill all the male children and all the non-virgin women? If so, how do you reconcile your view with Jesus's teaching that we are to love, pray for, do good to, and have mercy on all people, including our enemies (Luke 6:27, 35–36)? If not, how do we continue to affirm that this passage is divine inspired and to make sense of it?

No! →

YES! →

*PROTECTION
LONGEVITY*

OFF SPRING AND WIVES HISTORICALLY PURSUED
VENGEANCE AGAINST THEIR CONQUERORS.

JESUS PORTRAYED JUDGEMENT (WHITE WASHED
TOMBS) AND PROTECTION/DEFENDING DESCIPLES
THAT ACCUSED OF WORK by PHARISEES

BOYD HAS ASSUMED GOD'S INTENT; MIND;
BIASEDLY THAT GOD MEANT FOR THE
SOLDIERS TO USE THEN, NOT PROTECT
THEM.

GOD DOES NOT SAY THE SOLDIERS SHOULD
TAKE ADVANTAGE OF THE WOMEN

GOD DOES SAY HE'S AVENGING HIS people,
HIS SERVANTS. SIMILAR INTENT SHOWN IN
JOHN 15:14

Here are some additional study questions to help silently engage with Greg's thoughts:

1. Have you ever honestly faced and wrestled with the dark, grisly nature of these violent portraits of God before now? If not, why not? If so, how were you able to come to terms with them?

   No - I assumed God has the authority to do what is said and I presumed I didn't understand the whole story or purpose of His actions

2. Have you ever been able or willing to describe actions ascribed to God as "morally awful"? If not, why not?

   No and I'm still not

   I don't have the mind or heart of God. I understand from the passage Boyd selected that God is avenging, protecting, and furthering a people He has sworn to...

   He demonstrates mercy + friendship towards those that obey + judgement and consequence to the offenders

Here are some questions to process as a group:

1. Have the violent portraits of God been an "elephant in the room" in your personal or church experience? Were they addressed at all? How so or why not? *I don't believe the consequences God promises are understood + therefore unexplainable justice demands judgement! REVELATION!*

2. Discuss why you agree or disagree with Greg that we need to be forthright in acknowledging that the OT contains portraits of God that are "ugly" and "awful"?

   UNBIASED EXPLORATION IS BEST... BUT MEANINGFUL RESEARCH LEADS TO CONCLUSIONS I'VE ASSUMED GOD HAS HIS REASONS — FAITH

3. How have these kinds of violent portraits of God in the OT impacted your reading of Scripture, your mental conception of God, and/or your relationship with God? More specifically, have the OT's violent depictions of God hindered your ability to fully trust that God is as beautiful as Jesus reveals him to be? *No*

   I'VE VIEWED THE OT & NT TO BE DEPICTIONS of GOD AS PRESENT: LAW & GRACE RECENTLY THE THOT of VIEW BOTH THROUGH CHRIST

4. What do you think, and how do you feel, about Origen's counsel on passages that are "unworthy of God"? How comfortable or uncomfortable are you with acknowledging that violent portraits of God are "unworthy of God?"

   I don't believe translators are inspired to accurately interpret the Hebrew or Greek... initially the original language was

5. What remaining questions and/or objections do you have concerning the material covered in this chapter?

   GOD is INSPIRED. TODAY, WE HAVE THE BEST UNDERSTANDING ACHIEVED by MAN. I believe by FAITH ALONE THAT OT REVEAL THE IMPACT of LAW. THE NT reveals GRACE + MERCY. I PRESUME IT'S POSSIBLE TO PRESENT A

15

QUESTIONS AND ANSWERS: Here are some questions Greg has received on this material followed by his responses:

Q1: Isn't it presumptuous to judge any action taken by an all-good God to be "morally awful"? Couldn't something be morally awful for humans to do but good for God to do?

A1: Unless God's goodness is analogous to what we mean by the word "good," we have no idea what we mean when we call God "good." Our profession of faith in God's "goodness" is thus devoid of meaning. Even more importantly, Jesus fully reveals the goodness of God, and it involves loving enemies and refraining from engaging in violence against them, not annihilating them. *But we accept God's "good" when introducing creation. Can we not derive an understanding of God's meaning.*

Q2: How can you confess all Scripture to be "God-breathed" and yet not feel obliged to accept what every passage of Scripture plainly says, however offensive it may be?

A2: I accept what every passage of Scripture plainly says, but what God intended a verse to say to an ancient audience may be different from what God intends a verse to say to those of us who know his true character in the crucified Christ. This is why New Testament (NT) authors often found a Christ-centered meaning in passages that the original audience couldn't have dreamed of. As we'll demonstrate in later chapters, when we read passages containing violent portraits of God through the lens of the cross, we can discern a meaning that the original audience couldn't have discerned, and this meaning discloses how these violent divine portraits point to the revelation of God in the crucified Christ.

I think ot people did know the true nature of God. He expected obedience. He gave them laws, when not followed brought consequence

16 — *We instinctively know good from bad whether we know the "law" or not*

RECOMMENDED RESOURCES: Greg recommends the following material that discusses various issues and perspectives on material covered in this chapter:

Baker, D. *God: The Most Unpleasant Character in Fiction.* New York: Sterling, 2016.

Boyd, G. *The Crucifixion of the Warrior God: Interpreting the Old Testament's Violent Portraits of God in Light of the Cross.* 2 vols. Minneapolis: Fortress Press, 2017. 1:279–333.

Bergmann, M., M. J. Murray, and M. C. Rea, eds. *Divine Evil? The Moral Character of the God of Abraham.* New York: Oxford University Press, 2013.

Campbell, M. M. *Light on the Dark Side of God.* 2nd ed. Caldwell, ID: Truth for the Final Generation, 2003.

Craigie, P. C. *The Problem of War in the Old Testament.* Eugene, OR: Wipf & Stock, 2002.

Copan, P. *Is God a Moral Monster? Making Sense of the Old Testament God.* Grand Rapids: Baker, 2011.

Cowles, C. S., E. M. Merril, D. L. Gard, and T. Longman III. *Show Them No Mercy: 4 Views on God and Canaanite Genocide.* Grand Rapids: Zondervan, 2003.

Eller, V. *War & Peace (From Genesis to Revelation).* Eugene, OR: Wipf & Stock, 2003.

Fleischer, M. *The Old Testament Case for Nonviolence.* Oklahoma City, OK: Epic Octavius the Triumphant, 2017.

Geisler, N. L. "Slaughter of the Canaanites." In *Baker Encyclopedia of Christian Apologetics,* 113–14. Grand Rapids: Baker, 1999.

Jenkins, P. *Laying Down the Sword: Why We Can't Ignore the Bible's Violent Verses.* New York: HarperOne, 2011.

CHRIST FULFILLED THE LAW... HE DIDN'T ABOLISH IT. IN fact God promises JUSTICE IN THE END! Why isn't accountable of people DIDN'T RECEIVE JUSTICE PRIOR TO CHRIST. THE LAW WAS broken AND CONSEQUENCES were experienced.

Lamb, D. *God Behaving Badly: Is the God of the Old Testament Angry, Sexist and Racist?* Downers Grove: Intervarsity, IL: 2011.

Lüdemann, G. *The Unholy in Holy Scripture.* Louisville: Westminster John Knox, 1997.

Seibert, E. *Disturbing Divine Behavior: Troubling Old Testament Images of God.* Minneapolis: Fortress, 2009.

Sparks, K. L. *Sacred Word, Broken Word: Biblical Authority and the Dark Side of the Bible.* Grand Rapids: Eerdmans, 2012.

Spong, J. S. *The Sins of Scripture: Exposing the Bible's Tests of Hate to Reveal the God of Love* New York: HarperOne, 2005.

Thompson, A. *Who's Afraid of the Old Testament God?* 4th ed. Gonzalez, FL: Pacesetters Bible School, 2003.

Week #1: Part II—The Unveiling: What God Is Really Like

When something is "unveiled," we are able to see it for the first time or see it in a new way. Unveilings can come as a total surprise and induce great fear, like when you move a piece of furniture and a spider appears. Or they can be greatly anticipated and release great joy, like when a bride's veil is removed during a wedding.

Unveilings often create different reactions in each person or group who experiences it. When election or trial results are unveiled, they inspire jubilation for some and great disappointment for others. When a portrait is revealed, it can be hailed as a masterpiece by one critic and completely dismissed by another. When a blockbuster movie is released, it can be hailed as a triumph or ridiculed as trash.

In this chapter, Greg helps us reflect on the manner in which Jesus's cross-centered life and ministry fully unveil the true, loving character of God and how this unveiling contrasts with the mere glimpses of truth that God's people had throughout the OT.

THE BIG IDEA: Jesus alone is the exact representation of God's character.

FINDING JESUS: "The Bible itself instructs us to *base our mental representation of God solely on Jesus Christ. . . .* [N]othing in Scripture should ever be interpreted in a way that *qualifies or competes with* his revelation of God." (*CV:* 20)

TERMS AND DEFINITIONS: Major concepts from this lesson include:

- **the "flat view" of Scripture** = a way of reading the Bible that places Jesus's revelation of God on the same level as all other biblical depictions of God. Reading Scripture this way forces us to accept that God is *both* the nonviolent, enemy-loving God revealed in the crucified Christ *and* the violent, enemy-destroying God portrayed throughout the OT.

- *lex talionis* = the "law of just retaliation" (see Exod 21:24; Lev 24:19–20; Deut 19:21) teaches that the severity of the punishment *must* correspond to the severity of one's crime. Note: it doesn't merely allow for an "eye for an eye," it *requires* it. Amazingly, this is a principle that Jesus specifically instructs his followers to set aside, authoritatively *replacing* "an eye for an eye, a tooth for a tooth" with "love your enemy and pray for those who persecute you."

REFERENCES AND REFLECTIONS

Here is a summary of Greg's main points from this chapter:

The Unveiling: "If John [the Baptist] is greater than all the prophets leading up to Jesus, yet Jesus's teaching carries more weight than John's, doesn't it follow that Jesus's teaching should carry more weight than everything the prophets taught prior to him?" (*CV* 18)

The All-Too-Common Montage: "It's impossible to exaggerate the importance of a believer's mental representation of God. . . . [I]t's a neurological fact that people who have a loving mental representation of God tend to have a greater capacity to think objectively about controversial matters and to make rational decisions than do people who have a threatening mental representation of God. . . . [T]he Bible itself instructs us *to base our mental representation of God solely on Jesus Christ.*" (*CV* 18–20)

The Only Exact Representation: "Jesus is what God looks like when there are no clouds in the way. . . . Jesus is the *total content* of the Father's revelation to us." (*CV* 21)

The Life and Subject Matter of All Scripture: "The only proper way to 'study the Scriptures diligently' is to study it in a way that discloses how *all* of it is about Jesus and thus in a way that leads to the *life* of Scripture. . . . [T]he most important question we must ask while reading any part of the Bible is: 'How does this passage of Scripture . . . testify to Christ?'" (*CV* 22–23)

It's All in Christ: "If *all* the *fullness* of *Deity* is embodied and disclosed in Christ, we are misguided to think we need to supplement what we find in Christ with what we find in the OT or in any other source. *Everything* we need to know and can know about God is found *in Christ.*" (*CV* 24)

Jesus's Repudiation of Aspects of the Old Testament: "It's clear that while Jesus regarded the entire OT to be God-breathed, as should his followers, he also possessed the authority to cancel, and even reverse, its teachings. Jesus viewed the OT as a divinely inspired authority that was *under*, not *alongside*, his own divine authority." (*CV* 29)

No More "Eye for an Eye": "While all Scripture is divinely inspired, our understanding of God's character must be based entirely on the person of Jesus Christ, and, for reasons we will [see in the next week's lesson], especially on Christ crucified." (*CV* 31)

As you consider Greg's thoughts, please read and reflect on Hebrews 1:1–3:

1. If the author of Hebrews is correct, how do you think this passage should affect our interpretation of divine portraits in the OT that contradict the Son's revelation of the Father?

2. Do you think that this passage leaves open the possibility that the OT's violent portraits of God are as accurate a reflection of God as is Jesus's cross-centered life and ministry? Why or why not?

Here are some additional study questions to help silently engage with Greg's thoughts:

1. When you think of God, what images pop into your head? Where do you think you internalized these images? To what degree do these images agree and/or conflict with the revelation of God in the crucified Christ?

2. Is it difficult for you to accept Jesus as the ultimate revelation of God, not seeing him as *one* revelation of God *among many others* that are *equally* valid or complete, but as the *only* revelation of God that is *fully* authoritative? If so, why do you think this is?

3. If you became fully convinced that God was fully revealed in the crucified Christ, how would it alter your mental picture of God? How would it change your thoughts on how God thinks or feels about you and the rest of the world?

Here are some questions to process as a group:

1. Were you taught to read the Bible as a "flat book" in which the OT's violent portraits of God were assumed to have the same authority to reveal what God is truly like as Jesus does? If so, did you find Greg's case for a Jesus-centered way of reading the Bible convincing? Why or why not?

2. In your church or faith experience, have you ever been encouraged to wrestle with the question, "How do these violent portraits of God point to the crucified Christ?" If so, how did you grapple with that? If not, why do you think that is?

3. How do you think the church *embracing* the violent portraits of God since the fifth century has affected the way Christians have related to God and responded to perceived enemies? If the church fully embraced the crucified Christ as the full revelation of God and as the model of love that all Christians are called to emulate, how do you think the church would look different than it looks today?

4. What remaining questions and/or objections do you have concerning the material covered in this chapter?

QUESTIONS AND ANSWERS: Here are some questions Greg has received on this material followed by his responses:

Q1: If Jesus's revelation of God culminates and supersedes all previous revelations, why do we even need the OT?

A1: Jesus's mission and identity are steeped in the OT, and it would be impossible to understand this mission and identity without it. Indeed, we can recognize Jesus's revelation of God as culminating and superseding previous revelation only against the backdrop of the OT. Trying to understand Jesus apart from the OT is like hearing the punchline of a joke without first hearing the set up to this punchline.

Q2: I was taught that what Jesus repudiated in his sermon on the mount was not any passage in the OT but simply misguided traditions that sprung up around those passages. What do you make of this teaching?

A2: *Some* of the things Jesus repudiated were traditions, but I frankly see no way to avoid the conclusion that Jesus was repudiating specific OT teachings when he (for example) instructed disciples to never retaliate (contra Exod 21:24; Lev 24:19–20; Deut 19:21) and when he taught that no food we eat defiles us (contra Leviticus 11).

RECOMMENDED RESOURCES: Greg recommends the following material that discusses various issues and perspectives on material covered in this chapter:

Boyd, G. *The Crucifixion of the Warrior God: Interpreting the Old Testament's Violent Portraits of God in Light of the Cross.* 2 vols. Minneapolis: Fortress Press, 2017. 1:35–140.

Chapell, B. *Christ-Centered Preaching.* 2nd ed. Grand Rapids: Baker, 2005.

Flood, D. *Disarming Scripture: Cherry-Picking Liberals, Violence-Loving Conservatives, and Why We All Need to Learn to Read the Bible Like Jesus Did.* San Francisco: Metanoia: 2014.

Goldsworthy, G. *Christ-Centered Biblical Theology: Hermeneutical Foundations and Principles.* Downers Grove, IL: IVP Academic, 2012.

———. *Gospel-Centered Hermeneutics: Foundation and Principles of Evangelical Interpretation.* Downers Grover, IL: IVP Academic, 2006.

Hays, R. *Reading Backwards: Figural Christology and the Fourfold Gospel Witness.* Waco, TX: Baylor University Press, 1993.

Jersak, B. *A More Christlike God: A More Beautiful Gospel.* Pasadena, CA: Plain Truth Ministries: 2016.

Knight, G. A. F. *Christ the Center.* Maryknoll, NY: Orbis, 2004.

Myers, J. *The Atonement of God: Building Your Theology on a Crucivision of God.* Dallas, OR: Redeeming Press: 2016.

Torrance, T. F. *Incarnation: The Person and Life of Christ.* Edited by R. T. Walker. Downers Grove, IL: IVP Academic, 2008.

Williams, M. *How to Read the Bible through the Lens of Jesus.* Grand Rapids: Zondervan, 2012.

Wright, C. J. H. *Knowing Jesus through the Old Testament.* 2nd ed. Downers Grove, IL: IVP Academic, 2014.

Wright, N. T. *The Day the Revolution Began: Reconsidering the Meaning of Jesus' Crucifixion.* New York: HarperOne, 2017.

Young, W. P. *Lies We Believe about God.* New York: Atria, 2017.

Zahnd, B. *Sinners in the Hands of a Loving God: The Scandalous Truth of the Very Good News.* New York: Waterbrook, 2017.

Week #2: Part I—A Cruciform Through-Line: The Centrality of Christ Crucified

When considering the word "love," it's important to define the term since it can mean vastly different things to different people based on any number of factors. C. S. Lewis famously wrote about *The Four Loves*, highlighting the various types of love expressed in Greek language and thought, and how they are philosophically understood and tangibly practiced. Others have expanded that list to six types of love, each with its own Greek word to help express its unique meaning and application.

The English language, sadly, is much more limited, with only one word to express all these (and other) different types of love, making it much more difficult to define and live out. Defining "love" is critically important, however, and nowhere is that more important than when we consider what is meant by "the love of God." Nothing else will shape our thoughts and actions more tangibly over time than our understanding of "God's love."

So what *does* "the love of God" *mean*? And what do we mean when we hear John proclaim that "God is love" (1 John 4:8)? People have understood this "love" in different ways throughout history, but the cruciform hermeneutic helps us see that there is no greater picture to define and illustrate the love that is God's very essence than Jesus's cross-centered life and ministry.

THE BIG IDEA: Christ crucified is the ultimate expression of God's character.

FINDING JESUS: "The cross is the unsurpassable revelation of God's love . . . the definitive revelation of God's cross-like, or *cruciform*, character." (*CV* 36)

TERMS AND DEFINITIONS: Major concepts from this lesson include:

- **through-line** = a theme/idea that runs from the beginning to the end of a book, film, or so forth

- **cruciform** = the shape of a cross; reflecting the self-sacrificial character of the crucifixion

- *kenosis* = emptying oneself of something; Jesus emptied himself of his "divine advantages" so he could become one of us (Phil 2:6–11)

- **incarnation** = Jesus entering the world as both fully God and fully human

REFERENCES AND REFLECTIONS

Here is a summary of Greg's main points from this chapter:

An Ambiguous Love: "Augustine . . . argued that we should interpret the Bible with a 'rule of love,' meaning that anything we find in the Bible that isn't consistent with love should be interpreted figuratively. . . . Unfortunately, Augustine defined love as an inner attitude that did not have any necessary implications for how we actually treat others." (*CV* 35)

The Supreme Revelation: "The cross is the unsurpassable revelation of God's love. . . . [T]he cross is the definitive revelation of God's cross-like, or *cruciform*, character. . . . In all eternity, no event could ever reveal God's true self-sacrificial character more perfectly, for God could never go further for the sake of love than he went on Calvary." (*CV* 36–37)

Glorifying the Father: "If Jesus is the center to which all Scripture points, then the cruciform character of God that was supremely revealed on the cross must be regarded as the epicenter of this center. And if all Scripture is about *Christ*, then all Scripture is more specifically about *Christ crucified*." (*CV* 38)

The Incarnation: "The incarnation anticipates the crucifixion, and the crucifixion culminates the incarnation." (*CV* 39)[1]

The Cruciform Kingdom: "Jesus bases his command to love unconditionally on the indiscriminately loving character of the Father, not on the worthiness of those we are called to love." (*CV* 42)

---

1. And, I should add, Jesus's resurrection validates both.

Paul's Cruciform Gospel: "Whenever Paul speaks of 'Christ,' he has Christ crucified in mind. . . . Paul actually equates the 'gospel' with 'the message of the cross,' using the two phrases interchangeably. . . . [I]f you understand the meaning of Jesus's crucifixion, you understand everything you need to know about God and about the gospel." (*CV* 44)

What All This Means: "God is *cruciform love*, and in him there is no noncruciform love at all. Which is to say, there is no aspect of God that is not characterized by the nonviolent, self-sacrificial, enemy-embracing love that is revealed on the cross. . . . [U]ntil we fully trust that God is as he's revealed to be on the cross and therefore stop trying to justify these violent divine portraits, the cross cannot function like Alice's looking-glass, reversing the violent meaning of these portraits to show how they bear witness to the cross." (*CV* 46–47)

As you consider Greg's thoughts, please read and reflect on 1 John 4:7–11 and Philippians 2:1–8:

1. If "God is love" and Jesus is the perfect revelation of God, what does love actually look like, in practical terms, based on these passages?

2. If God is love, is it ever possible for God to act in a way that is contradictory to such love? How do you think this relates to the "wrath of God" that we read about in Scripture?

3. If we believe God can act violently, in seemingly brutal, horrific ways, what is to stop us from thinking we can act in that same way, and be justified in doing so? And if we feel justified acting in these ways, how do we reconcile this with Jesus's unequivocal instructions to always love and do good to enemies?

Here are some additional study questions to help silently engage with Greg's thoughts:

1. What would you do if you knew you had the power to do anything you wanted? Would you have acted the way Jesus did when he had the power to do anything he wanted (see Phil 2:1–8; John 13:3–5)?

2. What problems result from defining "love" as an inner feeling that has no necessary implications for how we actually treat others? How do you see this truncated Augustinian concept of "love" played out in church history and today?

3. Is it hard for you to fully embrace the idea that "in [God] there is no noncruciform love"? If so, reflect on what it is that makes embracing this belief difficult and whether or not this thing that causes you to resist this belief is of God or not.

Here are some questions to process as a group:

1. To what degree do you think Greg succeeded in arguing that the cross is the center of everything Jesus was about and thus the epicenter to which all Scripture points?

2. How does the incarnation anticipate the crucifixion? How does the crucifixion culminate the incarnation? How does the resurrection validate both?

3. Why do you think it's been so hard for the church to fully trust the revelation of God in the crucified Christ and to apply this revelation to how we both interpret and apply Scripture as we seek to fully love God and love our neighbors as ourselves?

4. What remaining questions and/or objections do you have surrounding the material covered in this chapter?

QUESTIONS AND ANSWERS

Here are some common questions Greg has received on this material followed by his responses:

Q1: How can you claim Jesus was completely against violence when he used a whip to chase everyone out of the temple?

A1: John says that Jesus used a homemade whip to drive "sheep and cattle" out of the temple (John 2:15). Throughout history, cracking a whip to startle animals has been the primary means of controlling their movement. This passage only suggests that Jesus cracked a whip to cause a stampede, not to harm any animals, let alone humans.

Q2: If Jesus is opposed to violence, why does Revelation depict Jesus as engaging in a slaughter-fest when he returns?

A2: Revelation is an apocalyptic book, which means it communicates through symbols rather than literal depictions. And the most fascinating thing about Revelation is that, while John uses a good deal of violent imagery that he pulls from the OT, he masterfully subverts the violence of this imagery. For example, in Revelation 19, John depicts Jesus as a warrior wearing a bloody robe (Rev 19:13). In the OT, this same image depicts a brave warrior wearing the blood of enemies he's slain (Isa 63:2–6), but John depicts Jesus as being covered in blood *before* he goes into battle. What this imagery communicates is that Jesus wages war not by shedding the blood of others but by allowing his own blood to be shed by others. Something similar could be said for all of the violent images in Revelation.

Q3: I don't understand how the entire OT can point to the cross. How, for example, do the creation accounts in Genesis 1 and 2 point to Jesus's self-sacrificial death?

A3: At the very least, the entire OT points to the crucified Christ by virtue of the fact that the crucified and resurrected Christ culminates the OT narrative and fulfills everything the first covenant was about. The creation stories in Genesis 1 and 2 set the stage for the whole drama of the biblical narrative to be played as it moves forward to its culmination in Jesus's cross-centered life and ministry, which results in the whole creation being reconciled to God and every aspect of creation being reconciled to each other (Col 1:15–20). But there are numerous other ways different aspects of the OT point to the crucified Christ, though in *CV* I am focused only on how the OT's violent portraits of God perform this function.

RECOMMENDED RESOURCES: Greg recommends the following material that discusses various issues and perspectives on material covered in this chapter.

Bauckham, R. *God Crucified: Monotheism and Christology in the New Testament*. Grand Rapids: Eerdmans, 1998.

———. *Jesus and the God of Israel: God Crucified and Other Studies in the New Testament Christology of Divine Identity*. Grand Rapids: Eerdmans, 2008.

Boyd, G. *The Crucifixion of the Warrior God: Interpreting the Old Testament's Violent Portraits of God in Light of the Cross*. 2 vols. Minneapolis: Fortress Press, 2017. 1:141–228, 593–628.

Carroll, J. T., and J. B. Green. *The Death of Jesus in Early Christianity*. Peabody, MA: Hendrickson, 1995.

Cousar, C. *A Theology of the Cross: The Death of Jesus in the Pauline Letters*. Minneapolis: Fortress Press, 1990.

Dear, J. *The God of Peace: Toward a Theology of Non-Violence*. Maryknoll, NY: Orbis, 1994.

Eller, V. *The Most Revealing Book of the Bible: Making Sense Out of Revelation*. Grand Rapids: Eerdmans: 1974.

Gorman, M. *Apostle of the Crucified Lord: A Theological Introduction to Paul and His Letters*. Grand Rapids: Eerdmans, 2004.

———. *Cruciformity: Paul's Narrative Spirituality of the Cross*. Grand Rapids: Eerdmans: 2001.

Moltmann, J. *The Crucified God*. 40th anniversary ed. Minneapolis: Fortress Press, 2014.

Morgan-Wynne, J. *The Cross in the Johannine Writings*. Eugene, OR: Wipf & Stock, 2011.

Tomlin, G. *The Power of the Cross: Theology and the Death of Christ in Paul, Luther, and Pascal*. Carlisle, UK: Paternoster, 1999.

Torrance, T. F. *Atonement: The Person and Work of Christ*. Edited by R. T. Walker. Downers Grove, IL: IVP Academic, 2009.

Wright, N. T. *The Day the Revolution Began: Reconsidering the Meaning of Jesus' Crucifixion*. New York: HarperOne: 2016.

Week #2: Part II—Revolting Beauty: Learning to See the Cross as the Key

As we've said from the beginning, if we're ever going to figure out how all Scripture points to the character of God that was fully revealed in the crucified Christ, we have to figure out how to read and interpret the violent portraits of God in the OT. In this chapter, we learn to see the cross as the key that fully reveals God's character, that enables us to read all Scripture in light of its revelation, that helps us better understand how God "breathed" Scripture for us, and that empowers us to see that God has always acted to reveal his true character *as much as possible*, while bearing his people's sin *as much as necessary* to maintain his covenant relationship with them.

THE BIG IDEA: Focusing on the cross as God's definitive revelation is the key that unlocks the mystery of how violent divine portraits anticipate, and point to, this definitive revelation.

FINDING JESUS: "The key to unlocking [the] mystery [of how violent divine portraits point to the cross] is found in the cross itself—*if* we are willing to completely trust it to reveal what God is truly like." (*CV* 51)

TERMS AND DEFINITIONS: Major concepts from this lesson include:

• **literary crucifix** = a passage of Scripture that serves as a literary testament to God's willingness to humbly stoop to allow the sin and cultural conditioning of his people to act upon him as he bears their sin, just as Jesus did on the cross

• **direct revelation** = any divine portrait or teaching that directly reflects God's cruciform character as it is supremely revealed through the crucified Christ

• **indirect revelation** = any divine portrait or teaching that fails to reflect the cruciform character of God and that thereby forces us to exercise our cross-informed faith to see through the passage's sin-mirroring surface to discern "what else is going on" behind the scenes

REFERENCES AND REFLECTIONS

Here is a summary of Greg's main points from this chapter:

Step 1: How the Cross Reveals God: "The cross is for believers both the revelation of the revolting ugliness of our sin and the revelation of the supremely beautiful God who was willing to stoop to take on this revolting ugliness." (*CV* 53)

Step 2: Reading Scripture with a Cross-Informed Faith: "We should read Scripture expecting to find God sometimes revealing his beautiful character by stooping to bear the ugly sin of his people, thereby taking on a surface appearance that mirrors that sin, just as he does on the cross. . . . [V]iolent divine portraits become literary crucifixes that bear witness to the historical crucifixion when interpreted through the looking-glass cross." (*CV* 53–54)

Step 3: A Cross-Centered Conception of God's "Breathing": "Most Evangelicals assume that God's 'breathing' is a *unilateral* and *unidirectional* activity, which implies that nothing conditions what results from God's breathing other than God's will. This is why so many assume that, since God is perfect, whatever results from his breathing must also be perfect. So, they conclude, the Bible must reflect God's own perfection. This is nothing more than an unwarranted assumption . . . the Bible is infallible. . . . But the all-important question is, *what did God inspire the Bible to infallibly accomplish?* . . . God inspired all Scripture to point us to Jesus, and more specifically, to the cross that culminates everything Jesus was about." (*CV* 56)

Step 4: The Relational, Noncoercive God: "Since God will not lobotomize people to get them where he wishes they were, he must be willing to humbly stoop to relate to us *as we are* . . . [and] must patiently bear our sin as he continues to influence us in the direction he wants for us. . . . God has always been willing to allow the sin of his people—including their sinful conceptions of him—to condition how he appears whenever he breathes revelations of himself. . . . Moreover . . . God must always act by means of *influence* rather than *coercion*. . . . God has always *acted toward* people to reveal his true self *as much as possible.* But he also has always been willing to humbly allow his people to *act upon him* as he bears their sin *as much as necessary.* To the degree that any portrait reflects the cruciform character of God, we can consider it a reflection of God *acting toward* people [or: direct revelations]. . . . Conversely, to the degree that the surface appearance of a biblical portrait fails to reflect the cruciform character of God, we can consider it to be a literary testament to God's willingness to humbly stoop to allow the sin and cultural conditioning of his people to *act upon him* as he bears the sin of his people [or: indirect revelations]." (*CV* 58–59)

As you consider Greg's thoughts, please read and reflect on Jeremiah 13:13–14:

1. How does the depiction of God in this passage compare with the revelation of God in the crucified Christ? Can you imagine Jesus under any circumstances engaging in the actions that Jeremiah attributes to God?

2. How does this passage serve as a "literary crucifix" that bears witness to the crucifixion of Jesus?

Here are some additional study questions to help silently engage with Greg's thoughts:

1. Is there anything getting in the way of your ability or willingness to trust the crucified Christ to fully reveal God's character to you?

2. Do you agree that God acts *relationally* instead of *coercively*? Why or why not? What has been your personal experience? Have you ever felt coerced by God or by others claiming to speak for God? Is a truly loving relationship possible when coercion is present?

3. What's your reaction to this comment from Greg: "Shouldn't we expect that [like the cross itself] the Bible will also appear 'foolish,' 'weak,' 'lowly,' and 'despised' according to the world's standards of wisdom, strength, and perfection?" Do you need the Bible to be free of any and all human imperfection in order to fully trust its revelation of God's character in the crucified Christ?

Here are some questions to process as a group:

1. What gets in the way of trusting *Christ crucified alone* to reveal God's true character to us? Whatever these obstacles are, discuss whether you feel they are legitimate or not?

2. Are you persuaded by Greg's argument that if God breathed his supreme revelation by becoming a limited human being and then becoming the sin and curse of humanity, we should not assume that the Bible, which God breathed for the ultimate purpose of bearing witness to this supreme revelation, will be devoid of material that reflects the limitations, sin, and God-forsaken curse of humanity? Why or why not?

3. Given Greg's distinction between "direct" and "indirect" revelations, what aspects of the portrait of God found in Jeremiah 13:13–14 do you think reflect a direct revelation, and which do you think are indirect? Discuss how this distinction might apply to other violent or otherwise immoral portraits of God in the OT that come to mind.

4. What remaining questions and/or objections do you have concerning the material covered in this chapter?

QUESTIONS AND ANSWERS: Here are some questions Greg has received about this material followed by his responses:

Q1: It seems like God sometimes acts coercively, even in the New Testament. For example, in Acts 9 Jesus shows up in a vision, knocks Paul to the ground, tells Paul he's been persecuting him, blinds him, and then commands him to go to Damascus for further instruction (Acts 9:6–10). This looks much more aggressive than merely influencing people with love.

A1: There is no denying that the Lord took extraordinary measures to bring Paul into the kingdom, but there is no indication that God overrode his free will. To the contrary, Jesus instructed Paul to go to Damascus only after Paul responded to the vision and asked, "What shall I do, Lord?" (Acts 22:10). Moreover, when Paul later recounted his experience to King Agrippa, he told him, "I was not disobedient to the heavenly vision" (Acts 26:19), implying, obviously, that Paul *could have* disobeyed the heavenly vision. This clearly implies that God did not coerce Paul into the kingdom.

Q2: In Romans 9 Paul depicts God acting very "coercively," as you put it. Paul says that God "has mercy upon whomever he wills, and he hardens the heart of whomever he wills" (Rom 9:18). Paul then adds that out of one lump of clay, God makes some vessels "of wrath, fit for destruction" to contrast with other "vessels of mercy prepared beforehand for glory" (vv. 21–23). How do we make sense of this in light of your claim that God operates by means of influence rather than coercion?

A2: Yes, God has mercy on whomever he wills, and he hardens whomever he wills, but the question is: Who does God choose to have mercy on, and who does God choose to harden? And the answer given by Paul in Romans is that God has mercy on all who chose to believe, but he hardens the hearts of all who chose to disbelieve. Hence, Paul says that Jews were hardened "because of their unbelief" (Rom 11:20). Notice, these people didn't disbelieve because they were first hardened. They were hardened because they first disbelieved.

This relates to Paul's use of the potter/clay analogy. Whenever ancient Jewish authors use an analogy derived from the OT, it's important to check out how the OT author used the analogy, for NT authors typically assume this in their own use of the analogy. The only place where the potter/clay analogy is fleshed out in the OT is in Jeremiah 18.

Yahweh had announced that a judgment was coming on Israel because of its persistent rebellion, and many Israelites were thinking their fate was sealed. Yahweh thus took Jeremiah to a potter's house where he witnessed a potter trying to fashion one type of vessel, only to find that the clay wasn't cooperating. The potter therefore "reworked [the clay] into another vessel, as it seemed good to the potter to do" (Jer 18:4). It's apparent that the point of the potter/clay analogy isn't about the potter's unilateral control over the clay. It's rather about the potter's wisdom in responding to the kind of clay he has to work with.

Hence, the Lord goes on to tell the Israelites that whenever he declares he is going to judge a nation for its wickedness and that nation responds by changing its ways, the Lord will change his mind and bless rather than judge that nation. Conversely, whenever God declares he's going to bless a nation for its righteousness and that nation turns wicked, God will change his mind and judge rather than bless that nation (Jer 18:5–11).

In short, God is the potter, people are the clay, and God will fashion the kind of vessel that is appropriate, given the kind of clay he has to work with. And we are the ones who determine what kind of clay God has to work by our choice to be pliable or resistant to the potter's designs. In short, the point of the potter/clay analogy in Romans 9 is not about God's unilateral power over the clay but about God's wise flexibility in responding to the clay.

RECOMMENDED RESOURCES: Greg recommends the following material that discusses various issues and perspectives on material covered in this chapter:

Boyd, G. *The Crucifixion of the Warrior God: Interpreting the Old Testament's Violent Portraits of God in Light of the Cross.* 2 vols. Minneapolis: Fortress Press, 2017. 1:463–511.

———. *Is God to Blame? Beyond Pat Answers to the Problem of Suffering.* Downers Grove, IL: InterVarsity, 2003.

———. *Satan and the Problem of Evil: Constructing a Trinitarian Warfare Theology.* Downers Grove, IL: InterVarsity, 2001.

Jersak, B. *A More Christlike God: A More Beautiful Gospel.* Pasadena, CA: Plain Truth Ministries: 2016.

Myers, J. *The Atonement of God: Building Your Theology on a Crucivision of God.* Dallas, OR: Redeeming Press: 2016.

Reddish, T. *Does God Always Get What God Wants: An Exploration of God's Activity in a Suffering World.* Eugene, OR: Cascade, 2018.

Sparks, K. L. *Sacred Word, Broken Word: Biblical Authority and the Dark Side of the Bible.* Grand Rapids: Eerdmans, 2012.

Zahnd, B. *Sinners in the Hands of a Loving God: The Scandalous Truth of the Very Good News.* New York: Waterbrook: 2017.

PART II

Biblical, Historical, and Ancient Cultural Support

Week #3: Building on Tradition: The Old and The New

Christianity is, in many ways, an inherited faith. We don't simply get to make it up as we go along without any sense of rootedness in, or connection to, the past. That being said, two diverging-yet-equally-valid points come to mind.

As we wrestle with the traditions or teachings we have inherited, we sometimes come to realize that, while a given tradition or teaching may be valuable on some level, it may be incomplete on others. When that is the case, we are called to stand on the shoulders of those who have gone before us, using the foundation they laid to help us see further than they were able or willing to see, for whatever reason. At other times, we may *think* the tradition or teaching we've inherited is the only acceptable position in the church tradition, only to later learn that the church tradition is actually more diverse than we previously assumed.

The content of this chapter touches on both of these scenarios, as we see how the cruciform hermeneutic isn't a completely new approach to reading Scripture but strives to provide a more thorough, consistent expression of the long-and-widely-held belief that Christ crucified is the center piece of all Christian theology. And while this approach may initially appear to be "brand new" or to "come out of thin air," it's actually deeply rooted in practices of scriptural interpretation as old as Christianity itself.

THE BIG IDEA: Just because it's new to you doesn't mean it's untrue.

FINDING JESUS: "Once in a while, what is new to you *can* be true, and what is old has *not* yet been told, at least not for a long while. ... [This] proposal [that the crucified Christ is the center point of all Christian theology] is not nearly as novel as it may initially appear." (*CV* 63)

TERMS AND DEFINITIONS: Major concepts from this lesson include:

• **Conservative Hermeneutical Principle** = the decision to stick as close as possible to the originally intended meaning of a passage, departing from it only when there are compelling reasons to do so

• **Theological Interpretation of Scripture** = reading the Bible in a way that moves beyond purely humanistic methods of interpretation to embrace it's unique, God-breathed nature in an effort to recover our ability to discern God-intended meanings that go beyond the authors' original intended meaning

• **divine accommodations** = portraits of God that don't reflect the way God actually is but rather reflect the fallen and culturally conditioned way an ancient author viewed him

• **progressive revelation** = the discernible progress in God's self-revelation throughout the biblical narrative

REFERENCES AND REFLECTIONS

Here is a summary of Greg's main points from this chapter:

Part 1: The Tradition of Finding the Crucified Christ in Scripture: "[Martin Luther said] that all true theology should be, from beginning to end, anchored in the cross . . . [saying the cross is] 'the key hermeneutical principle in understanding Scripture.' . . . Luther argues that we should intentionally read all Scripture in a way that leads to the cross. . . . Unfortunately, Luther was far from consistent in the way he applied his cross-centered hermeneutic. . . . [I am simply attempting] to apply Luther's cross-centered hermeneutic consistently." (*CV* 64–65)

Part 2: Looking Beyond the Surface Meaning: "*We should interpret the OT through the lens of the cross instead of restricting ourselves to the authors' originally intended meaning.* . . . If we insist that the only meaning a passage can have is the meaning it had for the original audience, then [for example] Matthew [2:15] was grossly misinterpreting Hosea [11:1]. . . . The church always assumed that passages of Scripture can have meanings that go well beyond their plain sense. . . . [T]he original intended meaning of a passage should only be departed from when there are good reasons to do so. . . . [I]t is *the text* of Scripture that Jesus endorses as divinely inspired, not the relationship between the text and actual history. . . . Scripture derives its divine authority from Jesus, not from the degree to which it corresponds to someone's opinion about what happened in the past." (*CV* 66–69)

Part 3: The Relational Nature of God's "Breathing": "Though they haven't always thought about it consistently, theologians throughout church history have almost always assumed that God's breathing of Scripture is conditioned by the medium he breathes through. . . . God's breathing is not a unilateral activity . . . when God inspired biblical authors, he had to accommodate their cognitive limitations and cultural perspectives. . . . [As such] many of the portraits of God in Scripture reflect divine accommodations. . . . [F]rom beginning to end, all of our thinking about God should be anchored in the cross. . . . [In light of the historical evidence] I trust it is clear that my claim that God allows the spiritual and intellectual condition of those he breathes through to condition the results of his breathing is not at all novel. The only novel aspect of my proposal is that I am applying this understanding to the OT's violent portraits of God as a means of protecting the moral character of God as it is revealed on the cross and to disclose how these violent portraits bear witness to the cross." (*CV* 69–72)

Part 4: Progressive Revelation: "[It is] a widely shared conviction that there is a discernible progress in God's self-revelation throughout the biblical narrative. . . . God has always revealed his true character and will *as much as possible* while stooping to accommodate the fallen and culturally conditioned state of his people *as much as necessary*. . . . [If we insist that the portraits of God in the OT were accurate depictions of God] we must believe that, while God needed to progressively reveal himself to his people in a multitude of other ways, when it comes to understanding God's character vis-à-vis violence, no progress has ever been needed! . . . [But] it is on precisely this point that the true

God revealed in the crucified Christ most thoroughly *contrasts* with the way fallen humans have always tended to conceive of God . . . including, unfortunately, with the way most Christians have conceived of God throughout history!" (*CV* 72–75)

Part 5: A Reflection on Church History: "Christian theologians have always applied the concepts of divine accommodation and progressive revelation to explain a number of puzzling things in the Bible. . . . If my proposal to reinterpret Scripture's violent portraits of God strikes you as radical and novel . . . [it is because t]hese portraits have been taken at face value for the last fifteen hundred years! . . . [P]agans have always assumed that military victories go to the army with the stronger god. . . . [I]f you're going to help run an empire, you've got to be willing to use the sword [and] . . . as Christians acclimated to the use of violence [in the fourth and fifth centuries], the OT's violent depictions of God became less problematic . . . [and eventually became] positively *advantageous*." (*CV* 75–77)

As you consider Greg's thoughts, please read and reflect on 1 Corinthians 1:14–16:

1. How does this passage serve to illustrate the relational way in which Scripture is "God-breathed"?

2. What might the presence of such a passage in God's inspired Scripture tell us about God's character and priorities in communicating and interacting with us?

Here are some additional study questions to help silently engage with Greg's thoughts:

1. Compare Matthew 2:15's use of Hosea 11:1. Was Matthew's use of the text valid in light of Hosea's originally intended meaning? (See Greg's comments on *CV* 66.)

2. Do you agree with Greg's commitment to the Conservative Hermeneutical Principle? Why does Greg think this principle is important? Do you agree or disagree with him? Why or why not?

3. Are you able to "dare to believe that God really is, to the core of his being, as beautiful as the cross reveals him to be?" If not, why not?

Here are some questions to process as a group:

1. What are some examples of "divine accommodation" in Scripture?

2. What are some examples of "progressive revelation" in Scripture?

3. Does this way of reading and interpreting Scripture seem "radical" and "novel" to you? What are some of the implications for us as a church if we were to embrace this reading of Scripture?

4. What remaining questions and/or objections do you have concerning the material covered in this chapter?

QUESTIONS AND ANSWERS: Here are some common questions Greg has received on this material followed by his responses:

Q1: It seems to me that when Jesus or NT authors refer to people or events in the OT, they are expressing their confidence that the OT is reflecting accurate history. I thus don't understand how you can claim a narrative should be regarded as divinely inspired even if it doesn't accurately reflect what actually happened in the past?

A1: During the Renaissance and Enlightenment periods, Western people developed a critical historical mindset that only accepts that something is "actual history" if it can be supported by historical evidence. As a result, modern Western historical-critical Bible scholars work with two narratives when investigating Scripture. They work with the biblical narrative, but they also work with a narrative of "what actually happened," which they and other scholars construct on the basis of the available historical evidence. And the question these scholars always ask is: How much of the biblical narrative comports with, and/or conflicts with, their constructed narrative of "what actually happened"?

By contrast, Jesus and the authors of the NT were only interested in the biblical narrative, which they considered to be the inspired word of God. They didn't worry about how this inspired narrative corresponded to, and/or conflicted with, a different constructed narrative of "what actually happened," as determined by someone's assessment of the available historical evidence. In this light, I don't believe we should interpret their various references to people and events in the OT as though they were intending to weigh in on the critical questions raised by modern historical-critical scholarship.

Moreover, our confidence in Scripture's inspiration should be anchored in the testimony of Jesus, not in how well the biblical narrative does or does not comport with some scholar's constructed narrative of "what actually happened." So, even if we were to conclude that a certain story in the biblical narrative fails to align with a scholarly narrative of "what actually happened," this should not diminish in the least our confidence that this story is divinely inspired. Nor would it relieve us of our responsibility to make sense of the violent portraits of God found in that story.

Q2: You reject the classical view of God as timeless, immutable (unchanging), and impassible (above having passions or suffering) and instead argue that all our thinking about God should be anchored in the crucified Christ. But in this case, on what basis can you believe that God is omniscient, omnipotent, and omnipresent, since Jesus was none of these things? Similarly, doesn't your cross-centered approach require you to interpret literally portraits of God needing to ask questions or to travel to get to other places to find things out, since Jesus had to do these things (e.g., Gen 3:9; 11:5, 7; 18:20–21)?

A2: To say that all of our thinking about God should be *anchored in* the crucified Christ is not to say that all of our thinking about God must be *restricted* to the crucified Christ. It simply means that whatever else we learn about God from Scripture, creation, reason, or any other source, must be *consistent with* God's self-revelation on the cross.

On top of this, it's important to remember that Jesus is both fully God and fully human. While God is omniscient, omnipotent, and omnipresent, the Son of God set aside the exercise of these attributes to become fully human (Phil 2:6). So, while the Son is as much God as is the Father and Spirit, in his incarnate state the Son is limited in a way that the Father and Spirit are not. And this is why a strongly

Christocentric hermeneutic need not interpret portraits of God asking questions, traveling places to learn things, or being limited in any other way, any more literally than classical theologians do.

Having said this, since defenders of the classical view of God believe God is "above" time (atemporal), they must interpret all passages that depict God moving from the past into the future to be divine accommodations. Since they believe God is completely "above" change (immutable), they must also interpret all passages that depict God being affected or moved by what humans do as well as all passages that depict God changing his plans in response to changing circumstances to be divine accommodations. And since they believe God is "above" experiencing strong emotions or suffering (impassible), defenders of classical theism must also interpret all passages that ascribe strong emotions or suffering to God to be divine accommodations.

Since almost every biblical portrait of God depicts him moving from the past into the future, being affected by humans, and experiencing emotions or suffering, the classical conception of God requires its adherents to assume that most, if not all, biblical conceptions of God do not reflect the way God actually is, but only the limited way humans must experience and understand him. To know what God is *really* like, in other words, we have to consult classical theologians, not the Bible.

I submit that if we begin our reflections about God with the crucified Christ rather than with a presupposed philosophical conception of God that goes back to pre-Socratic Hellenistic philosophers, it would never occur to us to think that God's capacity to move from the past to the future, to experience certain kinds of change, to experience strong emotions, and to suffer, are imperfections. To the contrary, if God completely lacked these capacities, as the classical view of God insists, it is hard to see how God could be considered personal, let alone perfectly loving. And it's especially hard to see how God could become (note the verb) a human being and suffer and die on the cross. Finally, it's especially hard, if not impossible, to understand how Jesus's crucifixion could genuinely reveal anything distinctive about God, let alone be the supreme revelation of God, if God can never experience change or suffering.

Q3: You have a rather negative view of Constantine and of "Christendom." While I agree that the "Church Triumphant" sometimes engaged in some terribly unchristian behavior, such as the Crusades and Inquisition, some scholars have argued that Christianity would never have become a global faith were it not for Constantine's "conversion" and his offer of political power to the church, which birthed Christendom. In this light, couldn't one argue that your view of Constantine and of Christendom is overly harsh?

A3: We only know how things unfolded, not how things might have unfolded differently had people made different choices. So yes, as a matter of historical fact, Constantine's alleged conversion and the birth of Christendom led to Christianity becoming a global faith. But the church of Christendom relied heavily on the use of the sword to become this, and to this degree it can no longer be considered to be a reflection of the cross-centered kingdom movement that Jesus inaugurated.

Who knows how things would have gone had the church followed the example of Jesus and rejected the temptations to acquire the authority of worldly kingdoms and to advance its cause by relying on the power of the sword (Matt 4:8–9)? What we *can* be sure of, however, is that God would never have allowed his kingdom movement to completely die out. Indeed, we can be sure that this cross-centered kingdom movement will eventually encompass the entire world when Jesus returns.

RECOMMENDED RESOURCES: Greg recommends the following material that discusses various issues and perspectives on material covered in this chapter:

Athaus, P. *The Theology of Martin Luther.* Translated by R. C. Schulz. Philadelphia: Fortress Press, 1966.

Boyd, G. *The Crucifixion of the Warrior God: Interpreting the Old Testament's Violent Portraits of God in Light of the Cross.* 2 vols. Minneapolis: Fortress Press, 2017. 1:229–76, 2:641–700.

Dryer, E. A., ed. *The Cross in the Christian Tradition: From Paul to Bonaventure.* New York: Paulist, 2000.

Frei, H. *The Eclipse of the Biblical Narrative.* New Haven: Yale University Press, 1974.

Lubac, H. de. *Scripture in the Tradition.* Translated by L. O'Neil. New York: Herder & Herder, 1968.

Madsen, A. *The Theology of the Cross in Historical Perspective.* Eugene, OR: Pickwick, 2007.

McGrath, A. E. *Luther's Theology of the Cross: Martin Luther's Theological Breakthrough.* New York: Blackwell, 1988.

Maugans-Driver, L. D. *Christ at the Center: The Early Christian Era.* Louisville: Westminster John Knox, 2009.

Roth, J. D., ed. *Constantine Revisited: Leithart, Yoder, and the Constantinian Debate.* Eugene, OR: Pickwick, 2013.

Tomlin, G. *The Power of the Cross: Theology and the Death of Christ in Paul, Luther and Pascal.* Carlisle, UK: Paternoster, 1999.

Treier, D. *Introducing Theological Interpretation of Scripture.* Grand Rapids: Baker, 2008.

Wink, W. *The Bible in Human Transformation.* Minneapolis: Fortress Press, 2010.

Week #4: The Heavenly Missionary: Divine Accommodation

I've been buying and wearing eyeglasses from a very early age. I'm certainly not legally blind, but I know enough to know I'd be relatively useless without them. In the process of buying and wearing, however, it's really the wearing that's the most important part. I can buy corrective lenses all day long, but until I actually put them on and use them, they won't do me any good. Choosing to exercise our "cross vision" when coming to the text is very similar: it's one thing to have the theory in mind, but it won't do us much good until we start using it to help us read Scripture as a whole.

Amazingly enough, once we determine to do that and thus assume a cross-centered interpretation of violent portraits of God in the OT, we start to see a wealth of evidence throughout Scripture confirming the accuracy and value of this approach. And the more we anchor our understanding of God's character in the crucified Christ, the more we are able to see and embrace the Bible's consistent depiction of God as a "heavenly missionary" who stoops to take on the sin-mirroring image his people project onto him.

In this chapter, we will see how God accommodates his peoples' limited, fallen, and culturally conditioned views of him in an effort to maintain covenant relationship with them and to continue to further his historical purposes through them until he can fully reveal himself in the ultimate, nonviolent, self-sacrificial, enemy-loving revelation of Christ crucified.

THE BIG IDEA: God is a heavenly missionary who accommodates his people as much as is necessary while accurately revealing himself to them as much as is possible.

FINDING JESUS: "Insofar as [any passage of Scripture] is sub-Christlike, it must be assessed to be a divine accommodation." (*CV* 99)

TERMS AND DEFINITIONS: Major concepts from this lesson include:

- **heavenly missionary** = a way of describing how God is grieved but willing to accommodate his people's fallen conceptions of him *as much as necessary* while diligently working to reveal as much of his true character to them *as possible*

- **accommodation** = a compromise; a willingness to adjust or adapt as is needed

REFERENCES AND REFLECTIONS

Here is a summary of Greg's main points from this chapter:

Part 1: Introduction: "Given that God created people free and thus with the potential for love, he must work by means of a loving influence rather than coercion. God has therefore always worked to reveal as much of his true character and will *as was possible* while accommodating the fallen state of his people *as much as was necessary*—though . . . it certainly grieved God deeply to do so." (*CV* 84–85)

Part 2: Marriage: "Marriage . . . from the start, was for a man and woman to become 'one flesh' for life. . . . Yet, according to the Genesis narrative, it wasn't long after Adam and Eve's rebellion that polygamy shows up and becomes the norm. Curiously, God never once speaks out against the practice, even when leaders like Samuel, David, and Solomon acquire wives. . . . [2 Samuel 12:8 might] lead us to believe that Yahweh was perfectly happy with David's multiple wives. . . . Our heavenly missionary here appears guilty of condoning the sin of polygamy. . . . Behind Yahweh's guilty appearance [however], we should discern our heavenly missionary humbly stooping out of love to bear the sin of his people, despite the grief this certainly caused him. . . . God clearly is not an inflexible legalist! If people's fallen state makes his ideal Plan A unattainable, God bends his ideal and mercifully offers them a Plan B. . . . This accommodating behavior is precisely what the revelation of God's self-sacrificial, sin-bearing love on the cross would lead us to expect." (*CV* 85–87)

Part 3: Israel's Monarchy: "God originally wanted to be the only king humans submitted to, and he hoped his chosen people would model this ideal to the other nations by getting by without a human king. Unfortunately, there came a time when the Israelites grew fearful of threatening nations around them and began to clamor for the security they thought a human king would provide. . . . Once Yahweh decided to yield to his people's demand, the biblical narrative consistently depicts Yahweh as approving, working through, and blessing Israel's kings . . . [and] when the Israelites demanded a king, they were at the same time asking Yahweh to function like the gods of all those other nations. So when Yahweh acquiesced to the one, he was acquiescing to the other—or at least he allowed his people to view him that way. . . . The OT's many portraits of Yahweh as a king-approving deity are accommodations, and this supports interpreting the portraits of Yahweh as a violent divine warrior who fights with, and for, the king the same way." (*CV* 87–89)

Part 4: Animal Sacrifices: "Are we to believe that the God who is fully revealed in Jesus actually sanctioned . . . animal cruelty and enjoyed the smell of burning animal carcasses? Surely *something else is going on.* . . . People in the ANE believed their sacrifices were feeding the gods, and it was the sweet aroma of these burning carcasses that told them it was suppertime. . . . [Though the OT doesn't depict God as actually eating these sacrifices] it's also clear that the ancient Israelites were not ready to let go of the belief that Yahweh enjoyed their burning aroma. And since God will not coerce people into having true conceptions of him, the heavenly missionary accommodated this misconception, which is why it frequently shows up in the inspired record of God's missionary activity. . . . This practice did not originate with Yahweh . . . [who we later learn in Hosea 6 and Hebrews 10] actually despised [these types of sacrifices] . . . [and] just as later prophets made it unmistakably clear that Yahweh never actually wanted animals killed, Jesus made it unmistakably clear that Yahweh never actually wanted humans killed." (*CV* 90–93)

Part 5: The Old Testament Law: "We have compelling reasons to interpret the entire Mosaic law, together with the law-oriented portrait of God it presupposes, to be an accommodation. . . . Even the Ten Commandments reflect highly accommodating elements . . . [like] the common ANE assumption that women are the property of men. . . . While God obviously is opposed to all forms of coveting, the patriarchal manner in which this opposition is expressed clearly reflects a high degree of cultural conditioning that our noncoercive heavenly missionary had to stoop to accommodate. . . . [Scripture itself shows us] that there were aspects of the law that didn't please God but rather reflect him adjusting his will to the fallen state of his people . . . [and] with the coming of Christ, Paul could look back and discern that *something else was going on*: the law was a provisional accommodation that served to put us in custody and lead us to Christ. . . . So, if there was something wrong with the law-centered covenant, it follows that there was something wrong with the law-oriented portrait of God that this covenant presupposes. . . . And if the law was a mere 'shadow' that is rendered 'obsolete' once 'the reality' of Christ appears, doesn't it follow that the law-oriented portrait of God was a mere 'shadow' that was rendered 'obsolete' once the real character of God was fully revealed in Christ? . . . [A]ccommodating sin was a foundational aspect of the heavenly missionary's strategy in the OT. . . . If violent and otherwise dubious laws . . . are provisional accommodations, it follows that the portraits of God giving these laws are . . . as well." (*CV* 93–97)

As you consider Greg's thoughts, please read and reflect on Deuteronomy 25:11–12:

1. Knowing that Jesus is the perfect revelation of God, can you imagine Jesus approving of (much less giving) the command in this passage?

2. How does this passage illustrate God's "heavenly missionary" activity of "stooping" to accommodate his people's false perceptions of him?

Here are some additional study questions to help silently engage with Greg's thoughts:

1. Is the picture of God as a "heavenly missionary" helpful to your conception of God? Why or why not?

2. Which of the areas of "accommodation" discussed in this chapter is the easiest to wrap your mind around and why?

3. Which "accommodation" is the hardest to wrap your mind around, and why?

Here are some questions to process as a group:

1. On *CV* 98 Greg says, "insofar as any divine portrait is not consistent with [the revelation of God in the crucified Christ], fidelity to Christ compels me to see it not as an accurate depiction of something God actually did but as a reflection of something God's people at the time assumed God did." Does that conclusion make sense to you? Why or why not?

2. Do you agree with Greg's assertion that the "accommodations [described in this lesson] lend credibility to the claim that we ought to interpret the OT's violent divine portraits as reflecting the same sin-bearing activity of our heavenly missionary" that we find on the cross? If not, why not?

3. What remaining questions and/or objections do you have concerning the material covered in this chapter?

QUESTIONS AND ANSWERS: Here are some questions Greg has received on this material followed by his responses:

Q1: Habakkuk says that God's "eyes are too pure to look on evil," and God "cannot tolerate wrongdoing" (1:13). So how can God possibly compromise ideals to meet people where they are at?

A1: One could argue that Habakkuk only meant to say that God's eyes are too holy to look *with approval* upon evil or to tolerate *forever* wrongdoing. But for the sake of argument, let's assume Habakkuk meant that God literally can't look upon any evil or tolerate any wrongdoing.

As I've argued, we need to anchor all our reflections about God in Jesus's cross-oriented life and ministry. When we do this, we discover that Jesus not only had no trouble tolerating wrongdoing, he routinely fellowshipped with tax collectors, prostitutes, and others that religious authorities regarded as the worst of sinners (e.g., Luke 5:30, 7:34, 15:2). Even more importantly, on the cross, Jesus was made "to be sin for us" (2 Cor 5:21). Now, if Jesus, the perfect revelation of God, fellowshipped with the worst of sinners and even in some sense *became* our sin, I have a hard time accepting Habakkuk's opinion that God can't tolerate any wrongdoing or that he finds it impossible to look upon sin and evil. Not only this, but all of the accommodations discussed in this chapter serve to refute Habakkuk's statement.

In this light, I consider Habakkuk's statement to reflect his own somewhat mistaken conception of God's holiness. Yet, the thing about Habakkuk's statement that reveals God to me is that, rather than coercing Habakkuk to understand the true nature of his holiness, God patiently stooped to allow Habakkuk to see him the way he did and to thus have his perspective recorded in the narrative of God's missionary activity.

Q2: *It doesn't seem like the missionaries who accommodated female circumcision in your opening story are good analogies for the way in which the OT's violent portraits of God reflect divine accommodations. The missionaries never commanded anyone to circumcise girls and never actually engaged in this practice. By contrast, many portraits of God in the OT depict him actually engaging in violence or commanding people to engage in violence.*

A2: All analogies break down at some point. The point of this analogy was simply to communicate the truth that, like the missionaries in this story, God had to sometimes stoop to accommodate people's mistaken views of him if he hoped to remain in covenant with them and to eventually grow them to the point that he could reveal his true nature and will to them in Christ. And like these missionaries, this meant that God appears to condone activities he actually strongly disapproves of.

At the same time, it would be easy to stretch the analogy of the missionaries to cover the fact that many biblical portraits of God depict him commanding or engaging in violence. As I noted in *CV*, for the three years before the tribe was ready to hear the missionaries' true opinions about female circumcision, these missionaries could only make the best of a bad situation by acquiring anesthesia, pain medication, and better surgical knives for the girls. So, suppose that after setting up the machine that administers anesthesia to the girls, one of the missionaries said; "The anesthesia is ready." Since this tribe assumed that the missionaries condoned this ritual, however, what the tribesmen who were conducting the ritual would likely *hear* is: "The anesthesia is ready; *begin to circumcise the girls*." And had one of these tribesmen been recording in a journal everything the missionaries said and did, *this* is likely what they would have written down.

So too, when biblical authors depict God as commanding or engaging in violence, they are recording what they *interpreted* God to be saying and/or doing. But the way they interpreted what God said and did often says more about their fallen and culturally conditioned assumptions about God than it says about what God actually said and did.

Q3: You speak of the cross as God's ultimate accommodation of our sin, but isn't the cross God's judgment of sin?

A3: The answer is that the cross is both God's ultimate accommodation of sin and God's ultimate judgment on sin. The cross is God's ultimate accommodation in that it is the ultimate example of God entering into our fallen state to bear our sin and to love and accept us just as we are. Yet it is God's ultimate judgment of sin in that the Father allowed Christ to suffer all the death-consequences of our sin in our place.

RECOMMENDED RESOURCES: Greg recommends the following material that discusses various issues and perspectives on material covered in this chapter:

Balserak, J. *Divinity Compromised: A Study of Divine Accommodation in the Thought of John Calvin.* Dordrecht, Netherlands: Springer, 2006.

Benin, S. D. *The Footprints of God: Divine Accommodation in Jewish and Christian Thought.* Albany: State University of New York, 1993.

Boyd, G. *The Crucifixion of the Warrior God: Interpreting the Old Testament's Violent Portraits of God in Light of the Cross.* 2 vols. Minneapolis: Fortress Press, 2017. 2:701–63.

Lewis, C. S. *Reflections on the Psalms.* In *The Inspirational Writings of C. S. Lewis.* New York: Inspirational Press, 1991.

Niehaus, J. J. *Ancient Near Eastern Themes in Biblical Theology.* Grand Rapids: Kregel, 2008.

Sparks, K. *Sacred Word, Broken Word: Biblical Authority and the Dark Side of Scripture.* Grand Rapids: Eerdmans, 2012.

VanGemeren, W. *The Progress of Redemption: The Story of Salvation from Creation to the New.* Grand Rapids: Zondervan Academic, 1988.

Walton, J. H. *Ancient Near Eastern Thought and the Old Testament.* Grand Rapids: Baker Academic, 2006.

Wright, D. P. *Inventing God's Laws: How the Covenant Code of the Bible Used and Revised the Laws of Hammurabi.* New York: Oxford University Press, 2009.

PART III

The True Nature of God's Judgment

Week #5: Part I—Rorschach God: Whose Image of God to Trust?

In 1921 Swiss psychologist Hermann Rorschach created a test designed to examine an individual's personality characteristics and how they function emotionally. By having folks look at a series of ambiguous inkblot images, the Rorschach test sought to bring the viewer's thought process to the surface. How people interpreted the inkblots revealed much more about the viewer's mindset than it did about the actual images themselves.

How we approach and apply Scripture often functions in the same way, telling us a great deal about ourselves and our perspectives, but often revealing very little about the God who is fully revealed in the crucified Christ. The more we seek to root our understanding of God's character solely in this supreme revelation, however, the more we are able to see and embrace the Bible's consistent depiction of God as a "heavenly missionary" who stoops to take on the sin-mirroring image that his people place on him as he accommodates their limited understanding of him, all in an effort to maintain covenant relationship with them and to continue to work in and through them until he can fully reveal himself in the ultimate, nonviolent, self-sacrificial, enemy-loving revelation of Christ crucified.

THE BIG IDEA: The way a person experiences God often reflects their preconception of God as well as the spiritual condition of their heart.

FINDING JESUS: "What people see and hear is strongly conditioned by what they expect to see and hear. . . . [P]eople are only able to receive the truth about God to the degree that their innermost hearts are aligned with his character." (*CV* 105)

TERMS AND DEFINITIONS: Major concepts from this lesson include:

• **projection** = when people project their desires, fears, motives, and expectations on to other people and/or circumstances; in this context, the phenomenon of people projecting their fallen and culturally conditioned preconceptions onto God

• **Rorschach test** = a test developed by Hermann Rorschach in 1921 to evaluate people's mental health; subjects stare at ambiguously shaped inkblots and report what they see

REFERENCES AND REFLECTIONS

Here is a summary of Greg's main points from this chapter:

Seeing What Our Hearts Allow Us to See: "What people see and hear is strongly conditioned by what they expect to see and hear. Along the same lines, people are only able to receive the truth about God to the degree that their innermost hearts are aligned with his character. . . . In this light, it is significant that the Bible repeatedly stresses that the Israelites were a stiff-necked people who continually resisted the Spirit and broke God's heart. . . . [According to the author of 2 Samuel 22:26–27] God appears faithful, blameless, and pure insofar as people's hearts and minds are faithful, blameless, and pure. But God appears in twisted ways insofar as people's hearts and minds are twisted. . . . The way God appears to people says at least as much about *them* as it does about *God* . . . insofar as people have twisted hearts and minds that suppress God's Spirit, they inevitably understand and experience God in ways that reflect their own twisted hearts and minds." (*CV* 105–6)

Making God in Our Own Image: "When Paul . . . defines the power of God as the self-sacrificial love revealed on the weak-looking cross (1 Cor 1:18, 30), you know this message had to be from God because it's not the kind of thing humans would ever make up on their own! In fact, it flatly contradicts the kind of coercive power people have typically ascribed to God/gods throughout history—including . . . most of church history. (*CV* 107)

Adjustments from God's Side: "Scripture indicates that, out of love for his people, God doesn't reveal more of himself than his people can handle . . . [and God is willing] to adjust his revelation to the low spiritual condition of people. . . . So the way people experience and understand God is conditioned both by the spiritual condition of their heart and by how much God withholds for their own good." (*CV* 108–9)

Reflections of the Anti-Violent God: "God's original plan was for the whole creation to be free of violence. This means that all violence among humans and within the animal kingdom is the result of something gone wrong. . . . [W]henever there is violence in God's creation, it is an indication that the true knowledge of the Lord is absent. *That* surely is significant as we consider Scripture's violent portraits of God. . . . [As we see in Psalm 46:9] God is indeed a heavenly warrior, but he is a warrior who 'fights for peace.' . . . In the words of James [4:1], violence is always the outgrowth 'of the desires that battle within [us].' . . . It never originates in the heart of God. . . . [E]very time the Israelites wielded the sword, we should see this as evidence that they were not placing their complete trust in Yahweh and were not filled with the true knowledge of the Lord. And note, this implies that the same holds true every time the ancient Israelites conceived of Yahweh as a violent ANE warrior deity who engages in violence and/or commands them to engage in violence." (*CV* 110–13)

An Abandoned Nonviolent Plan: "[As we see in Exodus 23:28–30, God had a plan to get] the indigenous population of Canaan to slowly migrate off the land on their own by making it unpleasantly pesky. . . . [And in Leviticus 18:24–25, we see that] the Lord decided he would allow the defilement of the Canaanites to render their land temporarily unfruitful so they would naturally migrate to greener pastures. . . . So . . . what happened to these nonviolent relocation strategies? . . . [T]hroughout the ANE it was assumed that acquiring land from another nation meant that you had to conquer, if not exterminate, the people of that nation. And it was uniformly assumed that the job of your national deity was to help you do this. . . . [I]t seems these nonviolent plans of Yahweh were simply too foreign to the Israelites' culturally conditioned ears to hear. . . . [W]hen Yahweh *said*, 'I want my people to dwell in the land of Canaan,' what Moses's fallen and culturally conditioned ears *heard* was, 'I want you to slaughter the Canaanites so my people can dwell in the land of Canaan.' . . . [T]his tells us more about the character of Moses and the culture he was embedded in than it tells us about the true character and will of God." (*CV* 114–17)

Conclusion: "The Israelites only engaged in violence because they had an insufficient trust in Yahweh. . . . [T]he violent portrait of God giving this command [for genocide], along with all other violent depictions of God, are accommodations. Their ugliness tells us much more about the heart of the people God was striving to work through than they tell us about God. . . . [When interpreted through the looking-glass cross] these grotesque portraits become literary crucifixes that reflect, and point to, the historical crucifixion of the humble, sin-bearing, heavenly missionary." (*CV* 118–19)

As you consider Greg's thoughts, please read and reflect on Exodus 5:3:

1. According to Greg, where did Moses and Aaron likely get the idea that God would strike them with plagues or with a sword if they were unsuccessful in their mission?

2. How does that view of God differ from the revelation we see in Jesus Christ?

3. When compared with the revelation of God in Jesus, what are some "twisted conceptions" you might have of God? Where do you think those conceptions originated?

Here are some additional study questions to help silently engage with Greg's thoughts:

1. Many sources impact our view of God: parents, spiritual leaders, sacred texts, religious music, and so forth. In your own experience, which source do you find "competing" most with the image of God found in Jesus's cross-centered life and ministry?

2. Before reading this chapter, had you ever noticed God's nonviolent plans to move the residents of Canaan off the land so Israel could occupy it? Are you persuaded by Greg's explanation for the radical shift in strategies? If not, what do you think caused this shift?

3. History tells us that many white European Christians used a literal/flat reading of the Canaanite conquest to justify the violent conquest of North America at the tragic expense of native populations. In this light, are there any current situations you can think of where a literal/flat reading of Scripture may be leading some Christians to adopt un-Christlike attitudes and/or engage in un-Christlike actions?

Here are some questions to process as a group:

1. According to Greg, because God is noncoercive, we need to read Scripture knowing that much of what we will find will tell us more about the fallen and culturally conditioned hearts and minds of God's people than it tells us about the true God. How is this way of reading the Bible different from the way you've read it in the past? What challenges or concerns does it raise? What opportunities and advantages does it present?

2. Greg leverages Paul's words in Galatians 1:18 to say that "we should not only *not* believe Moses" when he reports that Yahweh commanded the Israelites to mercilessly slaughter entire populations, "we should regard his command . . . to be 'under a curse.'" Discuss what (if any) challenges you have considering God-breathed material to be under a curse. How do you think Greg would respond to these challenges?

3. What remaining questions and/or objections do you have concerning the material covered in this chapter?

QUESTIONS AND ANSWERS: Here are some questions Greg has received on this material followed by his responses:

Q1: The Bible describes Moses as a friend of Yahweh who met with him "face-to-face" (Exod 33:11). In this light, it's hard for me to believe that Moses heard Yahweh wrongly or, if he did, that Yahweh couldn't have simply corrected him.

A1: When Moses asked to see Yahweh's glory, Yahweh replied that no one could see this and live. Moses was thus only allowed to see the backside of God (Exod 33:23). Only when God became a human and gave his life for us on the cross were people able to see the glory of God and remain alive (John 1:18). In this light, I think we should take care not to read too much into the several biblical reports that Moses fellowshipped with God "face-to-face."

However we understand this unique relationship, I see no reason to think it meant that Moses was incapable of misinterpreting God or of having false conceptions of God. Think about how the disciples misinterpreted Jesus, despite the fact that for three years they spent every day having a "face-to-face" relationship with him. For example, despite the fact that Jesus had repeatedly told his disciples about the need for him to go to Jerusalem and give his life as a ransom for many, these disciples were nevertheless utterly dismayed when it happened, for Jesus's teaching ran directly counter to their preconceptions of what the messiah was supposed to do.

Clearly, having a "face-to-face" relationship with God doesn't necessarily remove deeply held preconceptions that influence how people interpret what they see and hear. And unless God is going to resort to performing lobotomies on people to coerce them into hearing him correctly—which, I argue, God is never willing to do—God must humbly accommodate the way even his closest friends misunderstand and misconceive him.

This is confirmed, in my opinion, by the fact that Yahweh's plans for his children to enter the promised land nonviolently fell on deaf ears, as is evidenced by the simple fact that these plans were never enacted. According to the biblical tradition, Moses not only heard these plans, they were actually given *through him*. And yet it was Moses who reported that Yahweh was commanding the Israelites to show no mercy and to utterly devote to destruction the entire indigenous population in regions of the land that Yahweh had promised the Israelites. It is a stunning testimony to the Rorschach quality of all of our encounters with God.

Q2: I always thought that what separated the Bible from other religious books was that, while other religious books usually get some things right and some things wrong, biblical authors **always got things right** *because God breathed through them. But if God needed to sometimes accommodate biblical authors' misconceptions of him, as you claim, I wonder why we should consider the Bible to be any more "God-breathed" than any other religious book that gets some things right and other things wrong.*

A2: What makes this question particularly interesting is that Paul informs us that God has always been at work in every human heart to get people to "search for God and perhaps grope for him and find him—though indeed he is not far from each one of us. For 'in him we live and move and have our being,'" (Acts 17:28–29). Given this fact, it shouldn't surprise us that we sometimes find non-Christian religious writings that depict God and/or humans in ways that approximate what is revealed in the crucified Christ and expounded upon throughout the NT. With the crucified Christ as our ultimate criterion, we can assess the holy books of the world's religions and determine the degree to which God's Spirit managed to break through the fallen and culturally conditioned heart and mind of any religious author or religious group and the degree to which an author or group managed to suppress the Spirit's loving influence.

This is precisely how I am arguing Christians should interpret the Bible. But what sets the Bible apart from all other religious writings is that God alone explicitly breathed the Bible for the purpose of bringing people into a transforming relationship with the God who is ultimately revealed in Jesus's cross-centered life and ministry. Moreover, only the writings found within the canon of Scripture are essential to understanding who Jesus is, what he came to accomplish, and the life he calls disciples to live. And, finally, Jesus only endorsed these writings as the God-breathed word of God.

*Q3: If you're correct in attributing the violence of the evolutionary process and the violence that permeates nature today to the corrupting influence of demonic powers (**CV** 111n7), how could God say after the creation of humans that the whole creation was "very good" (Gen 1:31)?*

A3: Many scholars today and throughout church history have argued (correctly, in my opinion) that God's declaration that creation was "very good" doesn't mean the creation was *perfect* prior to the fall. The fact that Adam was told to "guard" (*samar*) the garden (Gen 2:15) and "subdue" (Gen 1:28) aspects of creation suggests that there were menacing forces in creation that humans would have to contend with, even prior to the fall. In fact, we encounter one of these menacing forces when we come upon the crafty serpent in Genesis 3.

In keeping with this view, I concur with those scholars who argue that God intended Eden to function as a sort of beachhead from which humans would go forth and subdue the rest of creation, which was yet entangled with the menacing forces that oppose God's creational design. By exercising loving dominion over the earth and animal kingdoms while subduing all that opposed God's design, humans were to bring about God's will "on earth as it is in heaven" (Matt 6:10). In this sense, some argue, the goodness of the original creation was more about the *potential* for creation to fulfill God's purposes than it was about the pristine state of creation prior to the fall (on this, see Dörnyei, *Progressive Creation* below).

RECOMMENDED RESOURCES: Greg recommends the following material that discusses various issues and perspectives on material covered in this chapter:

Boutange, J., and M. De Lara. *The Biased Brain.* New York: Springer, 2016.

Boyd, G. *The Crucifixion of the Warrior God: Interpreting the Old Testament's Violent Portraits of God in Light of the Cross.* 2 vols. Minneapolis: Fortress Press, 2017. 2:701–63, 920–1002.

———. "Evolution as Cosmic Warfare." In *Creation Made Free*, edited by T. J. Oord, 125–45. Eugene, OR: Pickwick, 2009.

Copan, P. *Is God a Moral Monster? Making Sense of the Old Testament God.* Grand Rapids: Baker, 2011.

Copan, P., and M. Flannagan. *Did God Really Command Genocide? Coming to Terms with the Justice of God.* Grand Rapids: Baker, 2014.

Cowles, C. S., E. M. Merril, D. L. Gard, and T. Longman III. *Show Them No Mercy: 4 Views on God and Canaanite Genocide.* Grand Rapids: Zondervan: 2003.

Dörnyei, Z. *Progressive Creation and the Struggles of Humanity in the Bible.* Eugene, OR: Pickwick, 2018.

Eller, V. *War and Peace from Genesis to Revelation.* Eugene, OR: Wipf & Stock, 2003.

Fleischer, M. *The Old Testament Case for Nonviolence.* Oklahoma City, OK: Epic Octavius the Triumphant: 2017.

Shermer, M. *The Believing Brain: From Ghosts and Gods to Politics and Conspiracies—How We Construct Beliefs and Reinforce Them as Truths.* New York: St. Martin's, 2012.

Week #5: Part II—Echoes of a Pagan Warrior: Reading the OT in Its ANE Context

Have you ever been reading through the OT and wondered what to do with some of the incredibly violent, macabre imagery ascribed to God? Presumably the answer is yes, otherwise you might not be going through this study guide right now! What are we to make of depictions of God in which smoke rises from his nostrils, he breathes fire out of his mouth, he throws lightning bolts as arrows down on enemies, to say nothing of images of God devouring his people, consuming his enemies, or crushing them like grapes so he and his people can dance in their blood to celebrate their victory? It's all so . . . brutal.

If you're like me, it might help to know that such imagery was common among ANE people, and it strongly reflects the culturally rooted perspective that everyone held at the time, including the authors of the OT. And while these portraits don't give us a "direct revelation" of the true character of God the way Jesus does, they nevertheless serve as "indirect revelations" bearing witness to the truth that God has always been doing what he did in a definitive way on the cross. Read through the lens of the looking-glass cross, depictions such as these become literary crucifixes that testify that God has always been willing to humbly enter into solidarity with people right where they are, bearing their fallen and culturally conditioned perspectives, thereby taking on an appearance that reflects the ugliness of that sin.

THE BIG IDEA: OT violence must be read and understood in its ancient historical context.

FINDING JESUS: "Nowhere is the cultural conditioning of the OT authors more evident than when they represent Yahweh as a violent divine warrior who battles Israel's earthly enemies. . . . Nowhere does the OT contrast with its surrounding ANE culture more than when it depicts God in Christlike ways." (*CV* 127, 131)

TERMS AND DEFINITIONS: Major concepts from this lesson include:

- *chaoskampf* = "conflict-with-chaos"; a major literary theme in ANE literature where deities defeat "the sea," "the waters," or "the deep" that represented personified cosmic forces that threatened the well-being of a given nation or the world at large

- **Anat** = an ancient Ugaritic goddess who was praised for her macabre, violent ferocity, accounts of which are clearly paralleled by Israel's later accounts of Yahweh's violent behavior in battle against Israel's cosmic or national enemies

REFERENCES AND REFLECTIONS

Here is a summary of Greg's main points from this chapter:

Yahweh Battles with Cosmic Enemies: "People in the ANE world, including the ancient Hebrews, believed that there were menacing cosmic forces that perpetually threatened the well-being of their nation and of the world. . . . [T]hey conceived of these cosmic forces as a threatening personified sea that they believed encompassed the earth. . . . Scholars refer to the many accounts we find in ANE literature of various deities defeating this sea as its *chaoskampf* ('conflict-with-chaos') motif. . . . The people of the ANE, including the ancient Israelites, also conceived of these threatening cosmic forces as cosmic monsters—most often as sea monsters [see e.g., Leviathan, Rahab]. . . . Jesus and the entire NT affirm the reality of the sinister cosmic forces that are mythically expressed by OT authors. It's just that, instead of talking about hostile waters or cosmic monsters, Jesus and the NT authors talk about Satan and principalities and powers." (*CV* 122–24)

Yahweh Battles with Human Enemies: "The people of the ANE . . . didn't clearly distinguish between earthly and spiritual battles. To the contrary, everyone in the ANE, including biblical authors, assumed that earthly battles are always wrapped up with spiritual battles. . . . [T]he Israelites were right insofar as they believed that cosmic foes threatened them, and that God battles the forces of destruction to protect people and to preserve the order of creation. But if we use the looking-glass cross to assess the culturally conditioned assumption of the OT authors that human foes are part of God's conflict-with-chaos and that it is appropriate for God's people to fight them as such, we must conclude that they were mistaken. . . . We are to battle cosmic foes, not human foes. And one of the primary ways we battle cosmic foes is by refusing to battle human foes, choosing instead to love and bless them." (*CV* 124–26)

Yahweh as a Warring Mountain and Storm Deity: "All ANE people believed their chief warrior god lived on top of a sacred mountain. . . . One of the most common images of warrior deities in the ANE depicts them descending into battle from their holy mountains while riding on storm clouds and throwing lightning bolts as arrows. We find this same imagery throughout the OT. . . . Every aspect of [the] depiction of Yahweh as a fire-breathing, smoke-snorting, cloud-riding, lightning-bolt-throwing, violent warrior deity has clear parallels with other ANE violent warrior deities. . . . [I]f we grant that this imagery is a culturally conditioned accommodation, *why should we not conclude the same about the violence that is associated with this imagery?*" (*CV* 127–29)

Yahweh and Anat: "It's not uncommon to find in ANE literature depictions of deities gloating over the grisly way they butchered masses of people. Not surprisingly, OT authors sometimes do the same thing. . . . Both Yahweh and [the Ugaritic goddess] Anat are described as leaving a bloodsoaked land with heaps of rotting corpses and piles of skulls in the wake of their ferocious warfare [e.g., Ps 110:5–6; Isa 34:3, 7; Jer 33:5]. And both are portrayed as crushing enemies like grapes in a winepress and joyously wading or dancing with their solders in their blood [e.g., Ps 58:10; 68:23; 110:5–6; Lam 1:15; Isa 63:3]. . . . Since ascribing macabre violence to their deities was the primary way ANE people exalted them, it's not too surprising that the

Ugaritic people exalted the ferociousness of Anat in this macabre fashion. What may shock some readers, however, is that the biblical authors exalt the ferociousness of Yahweh along similar lines." (*CV* 129–30)

Conclusion: "Nowhere does the OT contrast with its surrounding ANE culture more than when it depicts God in Christlike ways. Conversely, nowhere does the OT conform to its surrounding ANE culture more than when it depicts Yahweh as a violent warrior God." (*CV* 131)

As you consider Greg's thoughts, please read and reflect on Psalm 21:8–13:

1. Which verse parallels the ancient barbaric practice of military cannibalism, ascribing such actions to God?

2. Which words or phrases specifically reflect the ANE assumption that ascribing violence to God is a primary way of exalting him?

3. Can you imagine Jesus, under any circumstances, acting the way this author says God acts?

Here are some additional study questions to help silently engage with Greg's thoughts:

1. Greg argues, "We need a reliable criterion to distinguish between what OT authors got right and what they got wrong. On theological and ethical matters, this criterion is the cross" (*CV* 126). Do you agree? If not, why? Do you feel that no criteria is needed to distinguish truth from error, or do you think there is a better criterion?

2. Prior to this study, how did you process these Anat-resembling portraits of God in the OT? Do you find yourself processing them differently now? How so?

Here are some questions to process as a group:

1. What was your reaction when you first learned that the OT's portraits of Yahweh as a violent warrior closely resemble the way various warrior deities were depicted throughout the ANE? For example, did you experience relief, confusion, fascination, anger?

2. Read Psalm 18:1–19 out loud as a group and verbally call out together any words or images that reflect ANE perspectives in contrast to those that are consistent with the God revealed in the crucified Christ.

3. Greg says, "since God's revelation on the cross is the ultimate criterion by which we are to assess such matters, how can we avoid concluding that the violence associated with this imagery is at least as much a culturally conditioned accommodation as is the imagery itself?" (*CV* 129). Discuss whether or not you think this is a compelling argument, and why.

4. Given what we've learned about "literary crucifixes," why do you think God allowed such violent imagery to remain in the inspired record of his missionary activity? How does it point us to Jesus's cross-centered life and ministry?

5. What remaining questions and/or objections do you have concerning the material covered in this chapter?

QUESTIONS AND ANSWERS: Here are some questions Greg has received on this material followed by his responses:

Q1: I'm having a bit of a hard time accepting that God expected people after Christ to look through the surface of the OT's violent portraits of God to see him stooping to bear the sin of his people. Since God allowed people in the OT to believe that he was capable of engaging in grotesque violence, and since he allowed them to incorporate these false beliefs into the biblical narrative, it seems God could hardly blame people today for naively accepting these ancient beliefs are true.

A1: If it seems like too much for God to ask people after Christ to not accept violent portraits of God at face value, I suspect this is simply because we are so accustomed to *not* trusting that Jesus's cross-centered life and ministry fully reveal what God is like. Consequently, we are totally accustomed to accepting as accurate the violent portraits of God. Once we are completely confident that God is as beautiful as the crucified Christ reveals him to be, however, I submit that looking through the surface of these ugly portraits to see God humbly stooping to do what he does on the cross—bearing the sin of his people and taking on an appearance that reflects the ugliness of that sin—becomes perfectly natural.

To illustrate, once the tribe that used to perform female circumcision was able to embrace the gospel and see for themselves the sinfulness of this practice, would they not naturally understand that when the missionaries earlier appeared to condone this practice, they were actually stooping out of love to accommodate this practice until the tribe was ready to learn how these missionaries truly felt about it? The answer, I think, is obvious. So why is it any less natural for us to see what was really going on when OT authors depict God in violent terms now that we've learned from Christ that God's very essence is other-oriented, self-sacrificial, nonviolent love?

It is difficult, I suspect, only insofar as a person doesn't *really* trust that God is like this. Only when a person has lingering suspicions that God might actually be capable of engaging in the atrocious behaviors that OT authors ascribe to him will they find it hard to look by faith through the ugly surface of these portraits to see God engaging in the same sin-bearing activity that he does on the cross.

They key always comes back to: Do we really trust that Jesus is the full revelation of God? Having said this, I think it important that we give ourselves and give each other a lot of grace to wrestle with this paradigm shift. We need to realize that we've all been conditioned by a long and unfortunate tradition of *not* fully trusting in the revelation of the crucified Christ and thus of taking the violent portraits of God at face value. So, even after we decide to place our full trust in the crucified Christ, it takes some time to fully break old interpretive habits.

Q2: *I worry that you're leading people down a slippery slope. I get that certain things in the Bible are culturally conditioned and should now be discarded, like the practice of considering women to be the property of men or the practice of owning slaves. But when you claim that even some of the Bible's* **portraits of God** *might be culturally conditioned, it feels like the entire Bible is being thrown up for grabs. What is to stop people from dismissing anything they don't like on the grounds that the passage in question was just how people viewed things in those days?*

A2: First, my cross-centered interpretation of the OT's violent depictions of God as reflecting the cultural conditioning of biblical authors didn't create the issue of the "slippery slope." Rather, we have to confront this issue the minute we grant that the view of women as property or the practice of owning slaves or *anything else* in the Bible reflects an author's cultural conditioning. Since everyone grants that some aspects of Scripture are culturally conditioned, this is an issue everyone has to face, regardless of whether or not they accept the cross-centered approach to interpreting violent divine portraits.

Second, I would turn your objection around and ask: How can you *deny* that the OT's warrior portraits of God are culturally conditioned since they contradict the revelation of God in the crucified Christ and since we have a wealth of evidence that these depictions closely parallel—and sometimes copy exactly—depictions of warrior deities found throughout the ANE?

While we must always guard against our fallen inclination to base our assessment of what is and is not culturally conditioned in the Bible on our own subjective preferences, the interpretation of the OT's violent divine portraits that I'm recommending has the advantage of being anchored in an objective criterion that has nothing to do with our personal preferences. So, for example, while many today prefer to believe that God never judges people and thus tend to dismiss all passages dealing with "the wrath of God" as nothing more than reflections of ancient primitive beliefs, the criterion of the cross rules this out, for the cross reveals the true nature of God's "wrath."

RECOMMENDED RESOURCES: Greg recommends the following material that discusses various issues and perspectives on material covered in this chapter:

Batto, J. *Slaying the Dragon: Mythmaking in the Biblical Tradition.* Louisville: Westminster John Knox, 1992.

Boyd, G. *The Crucifixion of the Warrior God: Interpreting the Old Testament's Violent Portraits of God in Light of the Cross.* 2 vols. Minneapolis: Fortress Press, 2017. 2:746–63.

Clifford, R. J. *The Cosmic Mountain in Canaan and the Old Testament.* Cambridge, MA: Harvard University Press, 1972.

Cross, F. M. *Canaanite Myth and Hebrew Epic: Essays in the History of the Religion of Israel.* Cambridge, MA: Harvard University Press, 1973.

Day, J. *God's Conflict with the Dragon and the Sea: Echoes of a Canaanite Myth in the Old Testament.* Cambridge: Cambridge University Press, 1985.

———. *Yahweh and the Gods and Goddesses of Canaan.* Sheffield: Sheffield Academic Press, 2000.

Klingbeil, M. *Yahweh Fighting from Heaven: God as Warrior and as God of Heaven in the Hebrew Psalter and Ancient Near East Iconography.* Göttingen: Vandenhoeck & Ruprecht, 1999.

Kloos, C. *Yhwh's Combat with the Sea: A Canaanite Tradition in the Religion of Ancient Israel.* Leiden: Brill, 1986.

Levenson, J. *Creation and the Persistence of Evil: The Jewish Drama of Divine Omnipotence.* San Francisco: Harper & Row, 1988.

Miller, P. D. *The Divine Warrior in Early Israel.* Cambridge, MA: Harvard University Press, 1973.

Smith, M. "The Common Theology of the Ancient Near East." *Journal of Biblical Literature* 71, no. 3 (1953): 35–47.

Smith, M. S. *The Early History of God: Yahweh and the Other Deities in Ancient Israel.* San Francisco: Harper & Row, 1970.

van der Toorn, K., B. Becking, and P. W. van der Horst. *Dictionary of Deities and Demons in the Bible.* 2nd ed. Grand Rapids: Eerdmans, 1999.

Walton, J. H. *Ancient Near Eastern Thought and the Old Testament: Introducing the Conceptual World of the Hebrew Bible.* Grand Rapids: Baker Academic, 2006.

PART IV

Seeing *Something Else* through the Looking-Glass Cross

Week #6: Divine Aikido: God's Nonviolent Judgment

Movies were kind of a big deal to me growing up. Some of my clearest childhood memories revolve around my experiences going to a local theater or watching a movie on our basement VCR. As we come to this chapter, one movie memory in particular stands out: the day I saw *Karate Kid* for the first time.

Having just witnessed Daniel LaRusso's stunning victory over Johnny and the Cobra Kai dojo, I—and seemingly every other middle-school child leaving the theater—felt compelled to mimic the crane-like move Daniel employed to defeat his opponent and secure his tournament trophy. There was something about the grace of that move that was so appealing. But if I'm honest, I have to admit—I kind of liked the violence of it too. It felt good to see Johnny get kicked in the face after all the misery he'd visited on LaRusso throughout the movie. He got the judgment he deserved, and it felt like the violence was a rightful part of it.

As Greg points out in this chapter, that's pretty much par for the course when it comes to human ideas on how to mete out judgment, either on the human level or the divine. Throughout history we have resorted to violence to visit judgment upon the guilty or upon our enemies. Sadly, religious history shows how often we've assumed God needs to act the same way. But as we see in the revelation of God through the crucified Christ, that is a false assumption on our part, and one we desperately need to revisit.

THE BIG IDEA: God doesn't need to resort to violence to judge evil or sin.

FINDING JESUS: "The power and wisdom that God has always used to punish sin and overcome evil is the same nonviolent 'power and wisdom' he used to punish sin and overcome evil on the cross." (*CV* 137)

TERMS AND DEFINITIONS: Major concepts from this lesson include:

- **myth of redemptive violence** = the belief that violence is required to fix certain problems; for Christians this is often tied to the belief that God had to use violence to solve the problem of humanity's broken relationship with him

- **penal substitutionary view of the atonement** = a view of God's saving work on the cross that states (among other things) that God solves the problem of our estrangement from him by punishing his Son, violently slaying him in order to appease his wrath, which allows him to forgive us and to restore our relationship with God

- **Aikido** = a nonviolent school of martial arts in which practitioners never respond to aggressors by using their own aggressive force, but instead outsmart their opponents by using techniques that turn aggressive actions back on the aggressors, who thus end up punishing themselves

• *Christus Victor* = a view that holds that the central thing God accomplished on the cross was defeating Satan and freeing humanity and the whole creation from his corrupting reign

REFERENCES AND REFLECTIONS

Here is a summary of Greg's main points from this chapter:

An Unwarranted Assumption: "When it comes to understanding how God judges sin and evil, Christians have almost always assumed that God must do it the way humans have always done it and (not coincidentally) the way we've believed other gods do it: God must resort to violence. . . . I'd like to suggest that a better strategy would be to set aside everything we think we already know about the nature of God's judgment or God's wrath and resolve to 'know nothing . . . except Jesus Christ, and him crucified.' And . . . if we keep our eyes firmly fixed on the cross, we will see that, as a matter of fact, God never needs to resort to violence to punish sin or to overcome evil." (*CV* 137)

Judgment and Abandonment: "Prior to the eleventh century, most Christians believed that Jesus died not to free us from the Father's wrath but to free us from Satan's wrath. . . . The truth is that, according to the NT, God the Father didn't need to engage in any violence to have Jesus suffer in our place. Jesus certainly suffered a lot of violence, but every bit of it was carried out by wicked humans who were influenced by Satan and other rebel powers. The only thing God the Father did when Jesus suffered the judgment that we deserved was withdraw his protection. . . . Of course, in the process of withdrawing from Jesus to allow him to suffer, the Father was also abandoning him to bear the full weight of the world's sin and the full terror of the God-forsaken curse that comes with it. . . . This divine abandonment was the cup of God's wrath from which Jesus freely chose to drink. . . . *This* is the wrath that Jesus experienced, and it involved no anger or violence on God's part." *(CV 139–40)*

The Grief Behind the Wrath: "Jesus reveals that God is filled with grief when he sees that he must turn people over to the death-consequences of their sin. . . . Since Jesus reveals exactly what God is like down to his very essence, we must consider his intense grief over this impending judgment to be indicative of the grief God experiences whenever people come under his wrath. . . . We must envision the Father wailing rather than raging, and hopeful rather than vengeful." (*CV* 140–43)

Causing Evil to Self-Destruct: "First, the NT indicates that Satan and other fallen powers helped orchestrate the crucifixion. . . . Second, demons readily recognized Jesus as the Son of God, but they were completely mystified as to why he had come to earth. Third, Paul informs us that, had Satan and the rebel powers . . . understood 'God's wisdom,' they 'would not have crucified the Lord of glory' (1 Cor 2:7–8). . . . When we connect these three dots, we see that God managed to get the kingdom of darkness to orchestrate the very event that brought about its own demise." (*CV* 144)

Conclusion: "God wisely used the evil of Satan's loveless heart and inability to understand love to get him to orchestrate the destruction of his own evil kingdom. In other words, *God used evil to vanquish evil*. This was God's *Aikido strategy* in action. And since the cross reveals what God has always been like, we should assume that this is how the all-wise God has always punished sin and how he continues to vanquish evil." (*CV* 146)

As you consider Greg's thoughts, please read and reflect on 1 Corinthians 2:6–8 and Colossians 2:14–5:

1. According to Paul, how did God disarm the demonic forces aligned against Jesus?

2. Why does Paul say these these rebel "rulers" wouldn't have crucified Jesus had they understood the wisdom of God?

3. Why weren't the principalities and powers able to recognize that love was what motivated God to become a human?

Here are some additional study questions to help silently engage with Greg's thoughts:

1. Consider Jeremiah 48:31 and Hosea 11:8. What do these passages tell us about the heart of God when he sees that certain people must come under judgment?

2. Is it hard for you to think of God judging sin without using violence in the process? If so, why do you think that is?

3. Have you ever had to withdraw from someone out of love in order for them to experience the painful consequences of their decisions? What might your grief in that situation reveal to you about God's grief as he interacts with us?

Here are some questions to process as a group:

1. Which is easier to imagine: God using violence to judge sin or God working creatively to avoid the use of violence while still allowing people to experience divine judgment? Why do you think one option is easier to imagine than the other?

2. Greg offers brief descriptions of both the "penal substitution" and "*Christus Victor*" views of the atonement. Which one are you more familiar with? Do you share Greg's concerns with the "penal substitution" view? Why or why not?

3. What remaining questions and/or objections do you have concerning any of the material covered in this chapter?

QUESTIONS AND ANSWERS: Here are some questions Greg has received on this material followed by his responses:

Q1: If I release my pit bull knowing full well it will attack you, I am responsible for whatever harm it brings you. So too, if God withdraws his protection to allow wicked people or wicked spirit agents to harm people, how is he not still responsible for the suffering they inflict on people?

A1: If the analogy of the released pit bull accurately captured what goes on when God turns people over to the destructive consequences of their sin, then God clearly would be responsible for the suffering that comes about as a result. But I don't believe this analogy is at all accurate. It fails to capture the loving character and redemptive motive of God in withdrawing protection, and it fails to capture the fact that, unlike an innocent person being bit by an unleashed pit bull, the people being judged brought the destructive consequences of their sin *upon themselves.*

A better analogy would be a person who comes to the realization that they have been enabling a loved one to abuse alcohol or drugs by protecting them from the painful consequences of their behavior. If you've ever been in a situation like this, you know that your protection, though well-intentioned, was actually harming your loved one by allowing them to sink deeper into their alcohol or drug abuse.

In such circumstances, you really have no other choice but to withdraw your enabling assistance, as hard as this often is to do. So too, I believe the God of love revealed on the cross only withdraws protection when he sees that his loving and merciful protection of people is actually hurting them by allowing them to sink more deeply into their sin.

Q2: There is nothing my children could do to make me withdraw from them. Whatever they did, I would remain with them and would continue to love them. If God's parental love is greater than ours, how can he ever withdraw from us, his children?

A2: The Father didn't withdraw his love from Jesus on Calvary. He merely withdrew his protection to allow him to be crucified because it was not possible for the kingdom of darkness to be defeated any other way (Matt 26:49). So too, we have no reason to think that God ever withdraws his love when he withdraws his protection from people. To the contrary, God withdraws his protection from rebellious people precisely because he loves them too much to let them get irredeemably hardened in their rebellion. And he does this in the hope that these people will learn the hard way what they were unable or unwilling to learn the merciful way, when God was still protecting them from the damaging consequences of their choices.

Q3: Since God won't coerce people into believing the truth but rather accommodates their fallen and culturally conditioned perspectives as much as necessary, couldn't we consider all the passages that speak about God "withdrawing," "hiding his face," "turning people over," and so on to simply reflect the way ancient Israelites interpreted their misfortunes instead of accurate descriptions of what was actually going on?

A3: The primary criterion for assessing what is and is not an accommodation in any biblical portrait of God is the cross. As I've argued in this chapter, the cross came about by the Father withdrawing his protection to allow wicked humans and fallen powers to afflict and kill him as he stood in our place as a sinner. Since this is what God does in his definitive revelation on the cross, we have no reason to conclude that passages that depict God doing this with people are accommodations.

Not only this, but if God doesn't even withdraw protection when he sees he must bring judgment on people, then what *does* God do to bring about judgments? There is nothing less that God could do in response to sin than to allow people to go down their self-chosen path of destruction. If God doesn't even do this, however, then God does *nothing* in response to sin and evil in the world. This creates a deistic conception of a God who never really judges anyone, and this is fundamentally at odds not only with the God revealed throughout the Bible but also, and most importantly, with the God revealed in Jesus Christ.

RECOMMENDED RESOURCES: Greg recommends the following material that discusses various issues and perspectives on material covered in this chapter:

Boyd, G. *The Crucifixion of the Warrior God: Interpreting the Old Testament's Violent Portraits of God in Light of the Cross.* 2 vols. Minneapolis: Fortress Press, 2017. 2:767–850.

Fretheim, T. F. *Creation Untamed: The Bible, God, and Natural Disasters.* Grand Rapids: Baker Academic, 2010.

———. *God and World in the Old Testament: A Relational Theology of Creation.* Nashville: Abingdon, 2005.

Jersak, B., and M. Hardin. *Stricken by God: Nonviolent Identification and the Victory of Christ.* Grand Rapids: Eerdmans, 2007.

Krasove, K. *Reward, Punishment and Forgiveness.* New York: Brill, 1999.

Marshall, C. D. *Beyond Retribution: A New Testament Vision for Justice.* Grand Rapids: Eerdmans, 2001.

Miller, P. D. *Sin and Judgment in the Prophets.* New York: Scholars Press, 1982.

Patrick, D. *Redeeming Judgment.* Eugene, OR: Pickwick, 2012.

Schwager, R. *Must There Be Scapegoats? Violence and Redemption in the Bible.* Translated by M. L. Assad. New York: Crossroad, 2000.

Travis, S. H. *Christ and the Judgment of God: The Limits of Divine Retribution in New Testament Thought.* Milton Keynes, UK: Paternoster, 2008.

Week #7: Part I—Self-Punishing Sin: Divine Abandonment

Many years ago my wife, Jill, and I had the privilege of working at a PMIC (Psychiatric Mental Institution for Children) facility, caring for young boys who were court-ordered into the program based on behavioral problems brought on largely by "environmental" issues in their lives (e.g., experiencing abuse, neglect). Part of my role included sitting in with the boys on weekly anger-management classes (which remains one of the most valuable experiences of my adult life!). As part of anger management, the boys learned how to identify what "triggered" their anger, how their bodies responded in that moment, how it affected their thought process, what "thinking errors" they were prone to give in to as a result, and what "natural, logical consequences" they would experience as a result of their actions.

For instance, if they responded in anger by punching a wall, the natural, logical consequence of their action was the injury inflicted on their hand and the cost they would have to pay for whatever damage they caused to the wall. They might also miss out on a fun group activity because their injured hand wouldn't allow them to participate. In situations like this, no additional "judicial" punishment was necessary, as the "punishment" for their actions was inherent to their own actions. I didn't really have to do a thing.

In this chapter, we see that this is the predominate way God's judgment (sometimes described as "wrath") is depicted in Scripture. God never needs to engage in violence when he sees he must bring judgment on an individual or group. He simply needs to withdraw his protective hand, thereby allowing people to experience the destructive consequences inherent to our own sin. And whenever God sees he must do this, he does it with a grieving heart and with redemptive motives.

THE BIG IDEA: The punishment for sin is inherent to the sin itself.

FINDING JESUS: "Jesus never forced himself on anyone. Nor did Jesus ever retaliate against those who rejected him. . . . If we see the Father when we see Jesus (John 14:7–9), we have to consider Jesus's response to those who rejected him to be reflective of the way the Father has always responded to those who reject him." (*CV* 155)

TERMS AND DEFINITIONS: Major concepts from this lesson include:

- **judicial punishment** = a punishment that is imposed by an authority on a wrongdoer and that has no organic connection with the misdeeds that are being punished

- **organic punishment** = a punishment in which a wrongdoer is allowed to experience the destructive natural consequences of their misdeeds

REFERENCES AND REFLECTIONS

Here is a summary of Greg's main points from this chapter:

From Young Rocker to Thief: "The Bible generally construes God's punishment of sin as *organic* in nature. God doesn't *impose* punishments on people. The destructive consequences of sin are *built into the sin itself.* And this is why God only needs to withdraw and let sin run its self-destructive course when he judges people." (*CV* 148–49)

Divine Abandonment: "With the exception of its violent portraits of God, the Bible *always* describes God's judgments in terms of divine abandonment. For within the biblical worldview, to be separated from God is the worst thing imaginable. ... And the destructive consequences that resulted from this abandonment were identified as God's wrath." (*CV* 149–50)

The Organic Connection between Sin and Punishment: "Ancient Israelites generally understood the relationship between sin and punishment to be organic, not judicial in nature. ... God doesn't need to punish sinners by killing them, for when their sin becomes 'full-grown,' it naturally 'gives birth to death' [James 1:14–15]. ... [W]e must understand the organic conception of sin and punishment to be a *direct* God-breathed revelation while assessing the violent portraits of God to be *indirect* God-breathed revelations." (*CV* 151–52)

Self-Punishing Nature of Sin: "Another way the OT reflects the organic conception of divine judgment is by describing sin as inherently self-destructive ... people who persistently rebel against God eventually self-destruct." (*CV* 153–54)

God's Aikido Response to Evil in the NT: "When people decided they didn't want to follow [Jesus], what did Jesus do? He simply granted them their wish and let them go, even though it grieved him him to do so. Reflecting the noncoercive character of God, Jesus never forced himself on anyone. . . . If we see the Father when we see Jesus (John 14:7–9), we have to consider Jesus's response to those who rejected him to be reflective of the way the Father has always responded to those who reject him." (*CV* 154–55)

Three Questions about Divine Aikido—First: "While it is certain that persistent sin will *eventually* reap destructive consequences, the precise when, where, and how can be affected by any number of variables. . . . God doesn't micromanage the agents he uses to express his judgments." (*CV* 158)

Three Questions about Divine Aikido—Second: "So while God is willing to use people . . . who are already 'bent on destruction' to bring about divine judgments, I deny that God would ever *make* a person (or cosmic agent) become 'bent on destruction' so that he could use them for this purpose." (*CV* 159)

Three Questions about Divine Aikido—Third: "The default assumption of Christians should be that when groups or individuals suffer misfortune, it simply reflects the fact that God endowed human and angelic agents with free will. And because free will empowers these agents to exert a genuine influence over what comes to pass, for better or for worse, God cannot coercively intervene to prevent the harm they intend toward others. Of course, the all-good God is always *influentially* working to maximize good and minimize evil. . . . But however strong this influence is, it stops short of coercively overriding an agent's free will." (*CV* 159–60)

Conclusion: "The very narratives that attribute violent actions to God usually provide clues that this violence was actually carried out by other agents who were already bent on violence. Though the authors ascribe the violence involved in a divine judgment to God, the only thing God actually did is precisely what he did on the cross: with a grieving heart and a redemptive motive, he withdrew his presence to allow violent agents to do what they already wanted to do." (*CV* 160)

As you consider Greg's thoughts, please read and reflect on Psalm 7:12–16:

1. How is the Aikido nature of God's judgment expressed in this passage?

2. What ANE warrior imagery do we see in this passage? How does the Spirit break through to express how that imagery actually plays out in this scenario?

3. For further comparison, read and reflect on Proverbs 5:22, 11:5, 8:36, 21:7, 26:27.

Here are some additional study questions to help silently engage with Greg's thoughts:

1. How does Paul repeatedly describe God's judgment and wrath in Romans 1?

2. Is Paul describing judicial punishment or organic punishment? What aspects of Romans 1 lead you to this conclusion?

3. Have you ever experienced the "organic," painful consequences of a sinful or foolish pattern of choices in your life?

Here are some questions to process as a group:

1. Based on the revelation of Christ on the cross, how does God respond to those who reject him?

2. What do you think Greg means by the phrase "divine abandonment"? What form does this "abandonment" actually take? Is it a form of "rejection" or something else?

3. What remaining questions and/or objections do you have concerning the material covered in this chapter?

QUESTIONS AND ANSWERS: Here are some questions Greg has received on this material followed by his responses:

Q1: If the Father actually abandoned his Son on the cross, as you claim, then must you not accept that the Trinity was temporary fractured? Is this not an absurd conclusion?

A1: I completely agree that it would be absurd to suggest that the Trinity could ever be fractured, even temporarily. But the Father's abandonment of Jesus on the cross implies no such thing. Jesus was abandoned by the Father in the sense that the Father withdrew his protection from Jesus and in the sense that Jesus experienced the God-forsakenness that was inherent in the sin that he bore. This plan, agreed to by the Father, Son, and Spirit, not only didn't fracture the love that is the essence of the Trinity, it rather *perfectly reveals it.* For it was God's perfect love that motivated Jesus to go to the unsurpassable extreme of bearing our sin and God-forsakenness. Hence, as paradoxical as it sounds, the perfect love that unites the triune God was most perfectly revealed when Jesus experienced the God-forsaken consequences of our sin and thus cried out on the cross, "My God, My God, why have you forsaken me?"

Q2: What does Paul mean when he tells the Corinthians to turn over the unrepentant man (who was having sex with this stepmother) "to Satan for the destruction of the flesh" so that "his spirit might be saved on the day of the Lord" (1 Cor 5:5)?

A2: It's hard to know exactly what Paul meant when he expressed hope that this man would be saved as a result of Satan destroying his flesh. Most (but not all) scholars agree that the destruction of this man's flesh implies that he was going to die. So it seems Paul believed there could be something redemptive about the process of dying as a result of being afflicted by Satan. But since Paul doesn't elaborate, it's hard to know exactly how he envisioned this happening.

Q3: You claim that God's motive in allowing people to come under judgment is always redemptive. But how can a judgment be redemptive to the people who get killed as a result of this judgment?

A3: As I said in response to the previous question, it seems there is something that is at least potentially redemptive about the dying process when God withdraws protection and allows a person to be afflicted by violent agents. Moreover, I personally see no justification for the common Protestant assumption that God is done working with people when they die. To the contrary, I find a number of passages that seem to suggest that God continues to refine people's character after death (e.g., Matt 5:22–25; 1 Cor 3:11–15). If this is correct, then just because a person dies as a result of a divine judgment doesn't mean they are lost forever.

At the same time, while God has always been concerned with the salvation of every individual, in the OT God's redemptive motive was almost always directed at a national level. If God allows judgment to come on Egypt, for example, it is so Egypt will eventually be healed and brought into a right relationship with Yahweh (Isa 19:22).

RECOMMENDED RESOURCES: Greg recommends the following material that discusses various issues and perspectives on material covered in this chapter:

Baker, S. L. *Razing Hell: Rethinking Everything You've Been Taught about Hell and God's Wrath.* Louisville: Westminster John Knox, 2010.

Balentine, S. E. *The Hidden God: The Hiding of the Face of God in the Old Testament.* Oxford: Oxford University Press, 1983.

Bielby, J., and P. Eddy. *The Nature of the Atonement: Four Views.* Downers Grove, IL: InterVarsity, 2006.

Burnet, J. S. *Where Is God? Divine Absence in the Hebrew Bible.* Minneapolis: Fortress Press, 2010.

Fretheim, T. E. *Creation Untamed: The Bible, God, and Natural Disasters.* Grand Rapids: Baker Academic, 2010.

———. *God and World in the Old Testament: A Relational Theology of Creation.* Nashville: Abingdon, 2005.

Jersak, B., and M. Hardin, eds. *Stricken by God? Nonviolent Identification and the Victory of God.* Grand Rapids: Eerdmans, 2007.

Schwager, R. *Must There Be Scapegoats? Violence and Redemption in the Bible.* Translated by M. L. Assad. New York: Crossroad, 2000.

Travis, S. H. *Christ and the Judgment of God: The Limits of Divine Retribution in New Testament Thought.* Milton Keynes, UK: Paternoster, 2008.

Walls, J. *The Logic of Damnation.* Notre Dame: University of Notre Dame Press, 1992.

Week #7: Part II—Doing and Allowing: The Dual-Speech Pattern of Scripture

In the 1997 science-fiction film *Contact*, Dr. Ellie Arroway (played by Jodie Foster) uses a vast array of radio satellites to pick up a distant frequency that turns out to be a stream of communication proving humanity is not alone in the universe. At first the message, presented in a series of audible spikes representing prime numbers, seems totally indiscernible. As technology and expertise are brought to bear, however, incredibly detailed patterns start to emerge.

There's only one problem: they don't have the right primer (pronounced: primmer) to make sense of how all the data fits together. Eventually, of course, the primer is discovered, and when applied to the data from the message, everything comes together and a clear picture emerges. Data that previously made no sense finally comes into focus, and as it does all kinds of progress is made.

Throughout *Cross Vision*, Greg has been trying to help us see that, much like the pages and pages of confusing data Dr. Arroway and her team discovered in *Contact*—data that was critically important but ultimately unusable until the primer was found—the violent portraits of God in the OT are invaluable components of God's self-revelation to us, but it's only Christ's self-sacrificial death on the cross that can ultimately help us make sense of them. The cross helps us see things in ways we couldn't before. It unlocks mysteries that previously left us stumped (e.g., "How in the world could this violent portrait of God possibly bear witness to the love of God revealed in the crucified Christ?!") and helps us find patterns in the data we otherwise would have missed.

Rarely is that more clearly seen than in the passages of Scripture we're considering in this chapter. A pattern that was once present but hard to discern (before applying the "primer" of the cross) now shines through, revealing an aspect of Scripture we likely haven't seen before, but one that is invaluable in pointing us to the character of God so beautifully revealed in the crucified Christ.

THE BIG IDEA: Though ancient biblical authors often couldn't appreciate it, there is a world of difference between what God *allows* and what God *does*.

FINDING JESUS: "In short, what the true God actually did was humbly allow himself to appear guilty of things he in fact merely allowed. Yet, we will only be able to see this if we fully trust that the true God is supremely revealed in the crucified Christ and, therefore, that the true God would never be capable of crushing people like grapes in a winepress." (*CV* 169)

TERMS AND DEFINITIONS: Major concepts from this lesson include:

• **Scripture's dual-speech pattern** = Greg's description of how

Scripture often depicts God as simultaneously *doing* and *merely allowing* the same violent action

REFERENCES AND REFLECTIONS

Here is a summary of Greg's main points from this chapter:

You Killed My Son: "Whenever [OT authors operating in the ANE context] are crediting or blaming God when they depict him in violent ways, the very narratives in which they do this almost always contain indications that confirm that the violence they ascribe to God was actually carried out by other agents." (*CV* 163)

Who Killed Firstborn Egyptian Males?: "The very fact that [the author of Exodus's] own narrative indicates that Yahweh did not actually engage in the violence that he ascribes to Yahweh confirms that his violent portrait of God reflects his fallen and culturally conditioned assumptions about God. . . . [T]he presence of the portrait of Yahweh as a child-killing deity within the God-breathed witness to God's missionary activity serves as a permanent literary testimony to the truth that Yahweh has always been willing to stoop to accommodate the fallen and culturally conditioned way his covenant people viewed him, for only by this means could he hope to continue to influence them toward more accurate, and more beautiful, understandings of him." (*CV:* 164)

Who Is the Merciless Killer?: "Like all other ANE people, the Israelites assumed it was an insult *not* to 'credit' God with the violence that resulted from his judgment." (*CV* 166)

Who Crushes His Virgin Daughter?: "The atrocious portraits of God that fill Lamentations reflect Jeremiah's own ANE *interpretation* of how God was involved in this judgment, not the way God was actually involved." (*CV* 168)

Conclusion: "While OT authors thought they were exalting God by crediting him with all the violence that was involved in divine judgments, the looking-glass cross enables us to see that God was actually allowing sin to punish sin and evil to vanquish evil. And when interpreted through the looking-glass cross, all such episodes can be seen as signs that point to God's ultimate Aikido judgment of sin and victory over evil on Calvary." (*CV* 172)

As you consider Greg's thoughts, please read and reflect on the following passages:

1. How do we see the dual-speech pattern of Scripture present when we compare Deuteronomy 28:63 and 31:16–18?

2. How is this same pattern seen when comparing Jeremiah 33:5 and 34:2?

3. How about in Ezekiel 21:31a and 31b?

Here are some additional study questions to help silently engage with Greg's thoughts:

1. Greg quotes R. Schwager, saying, "For when God 'leaves humans to their own devices, they begin to destroy one another.' And *that* is what it means to come under the wrath of God" (*CV* 172). How is this understanding similar to, or different from, what you were taught about "the wrath of God"?

2. In light of Matthew 26:53 and Luke 23:34, how is Jeremiah 13:14 an example of what Greg calls an *indirect revelation*?

Here are some questions to process as a group:

1. Have someone read Exodus 12:1–23 out loud. Have someone else read Hebrews 11:28 out loud. How do we see Scripture's dual-speech pattern present in this situation? What is Yahweh depicted as simultaneously *doing* and merely *allowing*?

2. How is God's mode of withdrawing protection in Exodus 12 similar to the kind of judgment revealed in the death of Jesus on the cross?

3. What remaining questions and/or objections do you have concerning the material covered in this chapter?

QUESTIONS AND ANSWERS: Here are some questions Greg has received about this material followed by his responses:

Q1: When Old Testament authors mistakenly depict God as engaging in violence that he actually merely allowed, why didn't God just tell them "I didn't do that"? It doesn't seem that would be hard for God to do.

A1: Think how often Jesus told his disciples he had to go to Jerusalem, get arrested, and be executed. Yet, when he actually got arrested and crucified, his disciples were shocked and dismayed. Why? Because their preconception of the Messiah coming to defeat Israel's enemies and restore Israel as a sovereign, God-glorifying nation prevented them from truly hearing what Jesus was teaching.

God could have intervened and taken control of the disciple's brains so that they would hear Jesus correctly, but God always respects the personhood of people and thus refuses to lobotomize them into having correct views of him or into hearing him correctly. So, while God always influences people in the direction of the truth as much as possible, there comes a point where he must stoop to accommodate the mistaken ways his people view him and hear him.

Q2: The "dual-speech pattern" can be easily explained simply by accepting that God sovereignly controls all that comes to pass. For example, if God ordains all that comes to pass, one could say that the destroyer killed the firstborn throughout Egypt or that Yahweh killed the firstborn throughout Egypt, and both statements would be correct.

A2: That is certainly one way of explaining the "dual-speech pattern," but, among other problems, I would argue that this all-controlling model of divine sovereignty presupposes a picture of God that is radically at odds with the revelation of God in the crucified Christ. Moreover, if God actually did all the violence that OT authors ascribe to him, it is hard to see what it even means to say he merely allowed this violence to happen.

RECOMMENDED RESOURCES: Greg recommends the following material that discusses various issues and perspectives on material covered in this chapter:

Boyd, G. *The Crucifixion of the Warrior God: Interpreting the Old Testament's Violent Portraits of God in Light of the Cross.* 2 vols. Minneapolis: Fortress Press, 2017. 2:851–916.

———. *Is God to Blame? Moving Beyond Pat Answers to the Problem of Suffering.* Downers Grove, IL: InterVarsity, 2004.

Campbell, M. M. *Light on the Dark Side of God.* Caldwell, ID: Truth for the Final Generation, 2003.

Douglin, E. O. *God's Character: The Best News in the Universe.* Caldwell, ID: Truth for the Final Generation, 2005.

Fretheim, T. E. *Creation Untamed: The Bible, God, and Natural Disasters.* Grand Rapids: Baker Academic, 2010.

Week #8: Part I—Cosmic War: What's Going On Behind the Scenes

Human beings have always sought ways to explain the realities we deal with in the struggle of our human experience. Whether it's in response to the destruction wrought by a natural disaster or the suffering inflicted by another human, the human brain has always searched for a "big picture" framework to help us discern some kind of meaning behind the painful and apparently random madness that we so often experience.

In the ANE, people explained this random madness by appealing to a variety of supernatural forces and/or agents. They envisioned the earth as a plot of land surround by hostile water and menacing sea monsters. They considered the earth itself to be a malevolent cosmic agent or to have such an agent just underneath its surface, and they envisioned the heavens, the earth, and the underworld to be lorded over by an assortment of competing deities that could wreak destruction on the earth on a whim, whether by stirring up conflict among humans, afflicting us with plagues and other diseases, or by causing other kinds of disasters such as life-threatening floods, droughts, fires, or earthquakes.

The ancient Israelites largely embraced this ANE worldview, though their belief that one God (Yahweh) created all that exists—including all the other deities—and the emphasis they placed on the supremacy of this Creator-God, was unprecedented. By the time the NT was being written, the depiction of these hostile cosmic powers had changed somewhat. Instead of hostile waters and sea monsters, Jesus and the authors of the NT tend to talk about Satan, principalities and powers, and demons. But the basic understanding of the world as a warzone between God and cosmic forces that fight for good, on the one hand, and cosmic forces that have rebelled against God and that seek only to "kill, and to steal, and to destroy" (John 10:10), on the other, continued. Indeed, in the ministry of Jesus and the early church, this "cosmic conflict worldview" was significantly intensified.

While many contemporary Westerners, and especially most Western academics, dismiss this "cosmic conflict worldview" as a relic of humanity's mythological past, Greg argues that it is absolutely indispensable for a correct understanding of the ministry of Jesus as well as of the NT as a whole. Indeed, one of the central reasons the Son of God became human and offered up his life on the cross was "to destroy the one who has the power of death, that is, the devil" (Heb 2:14; cf. 1 John 3:8). And as we see in this chapter, Greg is convinced that we will never be able to understand how certain violent portraits of God point to the crucified Christ unless we push back on the anti-supernatural bias of our culture and accept, on the authority of Jesus, that our world is, in fact, oppressed by Satan and other rebellious cosmic powers.

THE BIG IDEA: Our world is a spiritual battlefield

FINDING JESUS: "The NT construes Jesus's crucifixion as the decisive battle in an age-long conflict between God and Satan. To interpret the OT through the lens of the cross . . . we must interpret it within a metanarrative of cosmic conflict." (*CV* 179)

TERMS AND DEFINITIONS: Major concepts from this lesson include:

- **Metanarrative** = a larger story that gives context to, and helps interpret, smaller stories

- **Cosmology** = the "big picture" people have of the cosmos and the place of humans in it

- **Myth** = a story that seeks to explain aspects of people's experience of the world, often by appealing to supernatural agents and miraculous events

REFERENCES AND REFLECTIONS
Here is a summary of Greg's main points from this chapter:

Discovering What Else Was Going On: "When the violence that an author ascribes to God can't be attributed to humans, it must be attributed to violent cosmic agents. And . . . this cross-centered interpretation finds a wealth of surprising confirming evidence in the narratives that contain these portraits." (*CV* 179)

A World Engulfed in War: "Jesus three times refers to Satan as 'the prince of this world.' . . . [W]hile Jesus and his followers believed God was the *ultimate* ruler over creation, these passages assert that Satan is currently the *functional* ruler over the earth.

... OT authors conceived of destructive cosmic forces as a hostile sea that encompasses the earth or as a threatening cosmic monster. Well, the NT refers to these same sinister cosmic powers with titles like 'rulers,' 'principalities,' 'powers,' authorities,' 'spiritual forces,' 'world rulers,' and 'elemental spirits.' ... Within the apocalyptic worldview that was pervasive among Jews in the first century and that is shared by the NT, it was understood that these cosmic agents had originally been given authority over aspects of nature and human society. Once they rebelled against God, however, they use this authority at cross-purposes with God to corrupt nature and society. This is essentially the perspective of the NT, though the NT is unique in its view that these rebel cosmic agents are ruled by Satan. . . . [T]he Gospels uniformly attribute afflictions not to the mysterious providence of God, as so many do today, but to the corrupting influence of Satan and demons. . . . [T]he supreme revelation of God's love on the cross was also his ultimate conflict with, and victory over, the powers of darkness. . . . [F]or people to fall under God's judgment, God needn't *do* anything. He needs to only *stop* doing something: namely, preventing the cosmic forces that are bent on destruction from doing what they are perpetually trying to do. And while the fallen and culturally conditioned authors of the OT were not above ascribing destructive acts to God, when we interpret their divinely inspired writings through the looking-glass cross, we will find a surprising amount of evidence that confirms that *this is all God ever did*." (*CV* 180–83)

The Destroying Angel and Korah's Rebellion: "On the basis of the cross, we must conclude that what actually happened [in Numbers 16] was that God, with a grieving heart, allowed evil to punish evil by turning these rebels over to experience the destructive consequences of their sin at the hands of agents who were already bent on violence. And since humans obviously didn't carry out this judgment, we must assume that it came about when God stopped holding back ever-present cosmic forces of destruction, just as he did with his Son on Calvary." (*CV* 184)

The First Group of Grumblers: "While the author of this narrative wanted to credit God with the violence of this judgment (Num 16:30), as any ANE person would, we can see that it wasn't God who opened up the earth to swallow people: they were swallowed by a menacing cosmic beast that is always hungry for someone to devour (1 Pet 5:8.) As an act of divine judgment, God merely stopped preventing this cosmic agent from doing what it always wants to do. . . . With the cross as our ultimate criterion, we must conclude that, while these [ANE] conceptions [of God, the earth, etc.] are mythic, the demonic realities to which they point *are not*. In other words, these mythic conceptions simply reflect the various ways ANE people thought about Satan and other malevolent angelic agents." (*CV* 188)

The Second Group of Grumblers: "Now, it's possible that this author is conceiving of Yahweh as a malevolent fire-throwing deity, similar to the way warrior deities are commonly depicted in ANE literature. . . . On the other hand, precisely because fire-throwing deities were common throughout the ANE, some scholars argue that this author was actually attributing the incinerating fire to one of these deities." (*CV* 189)

The Third Group of Grumblers: "In the OT, the concept of God's wrath typically refers to the dire consequences that naturally come about when people live in ways that violate the moral order of God's creation. Hence . . . wrath coming 'out from the Lord' need only mean that the Lord had decided to allow these people to experience the destructive consequences of their sinful choices." (*CV* 190)

Conclusion: "One could argue that Paul's introduction of a violent cosmic agent [1 Cor 10:10] as a means of distancing God from violence establishes a warrant for us to assume that destructive cosmic agents were involved in *all* divine judgments that don't involve the use of violent humans. And in making this observation, I am simply claiming that Paul was beginning to interpret the OT's violent portraits of God through the lens of the cross, along the lines I am advocating in this book." (*CV* 191)

As you consider Greg's thoughts, please read and reflect on Numbers 16:

1. There are three groups of "grumblers" described in this chapter. How does the author of Numbers describe how each group's destruction comes about?

2. How do these modes of destruction parallel ANE conceptions of cosmic agents?

3. What does Paul's reference in 1 Corinthians 10:10 tell us about how he himself was interpreting this OT story?

Here are some additional study questions to help silently engage with Greg's thoughts:

1. Do you accept the NT's perspective about cosmic agents like Satan, demons, and so on? Why or why not? If you don't accept this perspective, what do you think is going on when Jesus and the authors of the NT refer to them?

2. Is it possible (or beneficial) for us to accurately discern God's judgment through natural disasters or human-made tragedies? Why or why not?

3. If the gospels never attribute human sickness to God, but always to the corrupting influence of demonic forces, why do you think so many Christians nevertheless attribute such things to God's providence?

Here are some questions to process as a group:

1. What are some modern-day movie (or other fictional) examples of demonic forces similar to those in the ANE world?

2. How does the NT's depiction of the world as lorded over by Satan and other destructive fallen powers differ from the way you have tended to view the world? How might adopting the NT's perspective change how you live?

3. In what ways does the NT depict the ministry, death, and resurrection of Jesus as a battle against, and victory over, Satan and other cosmic forces of evil?

4. Does knowledge of ANE perspectives on menacing cosmic forces help your understanding of passages like Numbers 16? Does it bring clarity, or does it just seem incredibly weird?

5. What remaining questions and/or objections do you have concerning the material covered in this chapter?

QUESTIONS AND ANSWERS: Here are some questions Greg has received on this material followed by his responses:

Q1: Some scholars (such as Walter Wink) argue that the NT's language about Satan and the principalities and powers should be understood as referring to systemic aspects of society and/or to the collective "spirit" of people groups, whether of families, crowds, corporations, nations, or humanity as a whole. Wink and other scholars affirm that Satan and other cosmic powers are in some sense real, but they are real as extensions of ourselves, not as personal agents that exist independently of us. Wouldn't contemporary Western people find your thesis easier to swallow if you embraced this perspective?

A1: There is a great deal of truth in this perspective, for in the apocalyptic worldview that is shared by the authors of the NT, the cosmic powers were understood to have authority over systemic aspects of society as well as over aspects of nature. But Jesus and the authors of the NT clearly believed that Satan and other rebel powers are conscious agents that exist independently of humans. Since I have good reasons for believing Jesus is Lord, I don't believe I or anyone else is in a position to correct his theology, especially on a matter as foundational as this.

Not only this, but if Satan and other powers are simply mythological personifications of the collective "spirit" of people groups, they could play no role in our understanding of "natural" evil (viz. suffering brought about by forces of nature), which I consider to be a tremendous loss. They also could play no role in our understanding of depictions of divine judgments when no humans were involved in carrying out these judgments. This too I consider a tremendous loss.

Q2: Since Jesus was fully human, he shared the assumptions of the culture in which he was born and raised, including assumptions we now know are incorrect. Couldn't Jesus's belief in Satan, cosmic powers, and demons just be a reflection of his first-century cultural conditioning?

A2: I grant that, since Jesus was fully human, he shared the general assumptions of his culture, even some mistaken ones. For example, it seems Jesus shared the ancient misconception that people see not by having light come *into* our eyes but by light coming *out of* our eyes (Matt 6:22–23). But I find it very hard to accept that Jesus's belief in Satan and demons is one of these ancient misconceptions.

Yes, Jesus was fully human, but he was also a *perfect* human who taught only what he saw and heard from the Father (John 5:19–20, 30–31; 7:16–18; 8:38). Given how central Satan and demons are to Jesus's understanding of the world and his mission in it, I can only conclude that this belief was endorsed by the Father. If Jesus could have been mistaken about a belief as foundational as this one, one wonders if there is anything Jesus taught that couldn't have been mistaken?

On top of this, one of the ways we can determine whether a given biblical teaching is culturally relative or part of its timeless message is by observing whether or not the teaching is uniform throughout Scripture. For example, some passages condemn drinking alcohol (e.g., Prov 20:1; 21:17) while other passages speak in positive terms about it (Ps 104:15; 1 Tim 5:23). This diversity of perspectives suggests that whether or not it's okay for a person to drink alcohol depends on the culture and circumstances they find themselves in. But the understanding that the world is engulfed by cosmic agents who perpetually threaten it is found throughout the entire biblical narrative, which supports embracing this perspective as part of the Bible's timeless teaching.

Finally, I know of no compelling arguments to the effect that Satan and other cosmic powers don't exist independently of humans. This is nothing more than a modern Western assumption. However, there are compelling arguments *for* believing that Satan and other cosmic powers exist independently of humans. For example, as I indicated in my response to the previous question, I think it is very hard to reconcile the belief that the world was created by a perfectly benevolent Creator with the massive violence and suffering that permeates nature unless we accept that nature as we now find it has been corrupted by malevolent cosmic forces working at cross-purposes with God.

Q3: If Jesus came to bring an end to Satan and the entire kingdom of darkness, why does the world seem to be as messed up today as it was in Jesus's day?

A3: The NT adopts a bifocal perspective of Satan's defeat. On the one hand, it declares that the work of the cross brought an end to Satan's reign (e.g., Col 2:14). On the other hand, the NT depicts Satan's defeat as something that will only take place at the end of the age (Rev 20:10). In the meantime, Satan continues to carry out his destructive designs. For example, even after Jesus's resurrection, Peter describes Satan as "a roaring lion" that "prowls around, looking for someone to devour" (1 Pet 5:8) while John goes so far as to declare that, "the whole world lies under the power of the evil one" (1 John 5:19).

This is what is known as the "already-not yet" paradox of the NT. You can think of it along the lines of D-Day and V-Day in the Second World War. Historians generally agree that Germany *in prin-*

ciple lost the war on D-Day, June 6, 1944, when the United States and its allies defeated the Germans on Normandy beach in France. There was no way Germany could recover from this massive loss, though it took almost another year for the Germans to surrender on V-Day (May 8, 1944). Nevertheless, though Germany's defeat was now inevitable, there were still important battles that needed to be fought and multitudes of lives were to be lost on both sides as well as in Nazi death camps in the eleven months between D-Day and V-Day.

So too, we can think of the cross as the D-Day of God's defeat of the kingdom of darkness. The age-long cosmic battle that has engulfed our world was *in principle* brought to an end when Jesus died and rose again. But we have not yet arrived at V-Day, and in the meantime we must continue to struggle against Satan and other cosmic powers that continue to afflict us and our world.

RECOMMENDED RESOURCES: Greg recommends the following material that discusses various issues and perspectives on material covered in this chapter:

Arnold, C. *Powers of Darkness: Principalities and Powers in Paul's Letters.* Downers Grove, IL: InterVarsity, 1992.

Batto, B. *Slaying the Dragon: Mythmaking in the Biblical Tradition.* Louisville: Westminster John Knox, 1992.

Beilby, J., and P. Eddy. *Understanding Spiritual Warfare: Four Views.* Grand Rapids: Baker, 2012.

Boyd, G. *The Crucifixion of the Warrior God: Interpreting the Old Testament's Violent Portraits of God in Light of the Cross.* 2 vols. Minneapolis: Fortress Press, 2017. 2:1005–98.

———. *God at War: The Bible and Spiritual Conflict.* Downers Grove, IL: InterVarsity, 1996.

———. *Is God to Blame? Moving Beyond Pat Answers to the Problem of Suffering.* Downers Grove, IL: InterVarsity, 2003.

———. *Satan and the Problem of Evil: Constructing a Trinitarian Warfare Theodicy.* Downers Grove, IL: InterVarsity, 2001.

Day, J. *God's Conflict with the Dragon and the Sea: Echoes of a Canaanite Myth in the Old Testament.* New York: Cambridge University Press, 1985.

Fyall, R. *Now My Eyes Have Seen You: Images of Creation and Evil in the Book of Job.* Downers Grove, IL: InterVarsity, 2002.

Kallas, J. *Jesus and the Power of Satan.* Philadelphia: Westminster, 1968.

———. *The Satanward View: A Study in Pauline Theology.* Philadelphia: Westminster, 1966.

———. *The Significance of the Synoptic Miracles.* New York: Seabury, 1961.

van der Toorn, K., B Becking, and P. W. van der Horst. *Dictionary of Deities and Demons in the Bible*. 2nd ed. Grand Rapids: Eerdmans, 1999.

Wakeman, M. K. *God's Battle with the Monster*. Leiden: Brill, 1973.

Wink, W. *The Powers That Be*. New York: Doubleday, 1992.

Week #8: Part II—Creation Undone: The BIG-Big Picture

At the beginning of the last lesson we talked about how the human brain naturally seeks a "big picture" understanding of our experience. In this lesson we expand that concept a bit, as Greg discusses "the BIG-big picture," exploring not simply the meaning behind individual moments or events but the ultimate plan that God has for humanity and the whole creation.

To do so, we'll be discussing the Flood narrative from Genesis. Many people associate this story with cute Sunday-school drawings of happy animals marching two-by-two onto an undersized ark with Noah and his family smiling as they wave at the incoming animals. In reality, this story is *anything but* a children's story; it's a story about a divine judgment that brought about unprecedented death and destruction.

On the surface, this story is revoltingly ugly. If we exercise the same surface-penetrating faith that we employ to see Jesus's crucifixion as the definitive revelation of God, however, we can discern God humbly stooping to bear this author's fallen conception of God, thereby allowing himself to be depicted as causing a flood he in fact merely allowed. Not only this, but a careful reading of this narrative provides clues as to why Yahweh felt he had to go to the extreme of allowing the whole creation to become "undone."

THE BIG IDEA: The Flood was, above all else, a rescue mission of the entire creation project.

FINDING JESUS: "As God's revelation on the cross leads us to expect, God was once again using evil to punish evil as a sign pointing to, and a stepping-stone toward, his ultimate judgment and victory over sin and evil on Calvary." (*CV* 201)

TERMS AND DEFINITIONS: Major concepts from this lesson include:

> • *The Epic of Gilgamesh* = an ancient Mesopotamian work about a deity named Enlil who sends a flood because he is irritated by how noisy humans have become

> • **the deep** = while largely "depersonalized" in the Flood narrative, many scholars argue it should nevertheless be understood as possessing the same menacing character in this narrative that it has in the ANE conflict-with-chaos narratives, representing the chaos and evil that perpetually threatens God's creation

REFERENCES AND REFLECTIONS

Here is a summary of Greg's main points from this chapter:

Didn't God Love All the Animals?: "As I have stated several times, it is *the narrative* that is divinely inspired, regardless of what we think about the historical event it is based on." (*CV* 194)

As Humans Go, So the Earth and Animal Kingdom Goes: "First, it's important to remember that ancient Israelites viewed the world like a sort of 'spider web' in which everything was organically related to everything else. . . . Whenever humans, whom God entrusted to care for the earth and animal kingdom, push God away with their sin, the land and animals suffer as a result. Conversely, biblical authors never separate the salvation of humans from the restoration of the earth and animal kingdom. . . . [W]e should interpret the Flood narrative not as a judgment that God violently imposed on the earth but as an extreme example of what collective human sin looks like when God withdraws his merciful restraints to allow it to run its self-destructive course." (*CV* 195–96)

From Corruption to Destruction: "Second, we can see the organic connection between humans and creation in the way the author of the Flood narrative speaks about the corruption of humans and the destruction of the earth. . . . This narrative paints a picture of the God-commissioned rulers of the earth spiraling into an abyss of wickedness and violence and taking all that was under their authority down with them. . . . [W]hen God saw that his merciful striving [to restrain 'the deep'] had no hope of turning the earth's landlords around, he had no choice but to

withdraw his Spirit. . . . As always, God used evil to punish evil."
(*CV* 196–97)

The Agents of Destruction: "Third, while this author reflects his ANE cultural conditioning by crediting Yahweh with the horrendous violence of this judgment, it is remarkable that he never actually depicts God actively bringing it about. . . . The actual agents of the destruction, we see, were the floodwaters and the springs of the great deep, *not God*. . . . God's use of the cosmic waters to bring about this judgment was no different from the way he used nations that were 'bent on destruction' to judge Israel. . . . In short, the people in Noah's day experienced God's wrath in the same Aikido-like way Jesus did on Calvary."
(*CV* 197–98)

The Flood and the Undoing of Creation: "It's significant that the language of the Flood narrative parallels, in reverse order, the creation account of Genesis 1. The author is portraying the Flood as the undoing of creation. . . . In short, while God created the present world by constraining the hostile cosmic waters, he now allows the process to be reversed by lifting his restraint, thereby allowing 'the deep' to once again cover everything, returning creation to a state of being 'formless and void' (Gen 1:2). . . . In this light, I trust it's clear that the Flood was not the result of something God *did*, but of something God *stopped doing*. . . . When the One who perpetually restrains hostile cosmic forces as he holds all things together *refrains from these activities*, then, as a matter of course, all hell breaks loose. . . . As God's revelation on the cross leads us to expect, God was once again using evil to punish evil as a sign pointing to, and a stepping stone toward, his ultimate judgment and victory over sin and evil on Calvary." (*CV* 198–201)

The Spirit Breaking Through: "First, in nonbiblical flood stories, a god sends a flood in a fit of rage, and usually for petty reasons. . . . [Second,] the biblical account views the Flood as a necessary judgment that God reluctantly allowed only after he had spent centuries striving with humans to prevent it. Not only this, but the primary purpose of the Flood in the biblical narrative wasn't even to punish sin, but to *rescue God's creation project*." (*CV* 201–2)

As you consider Greg's thoughts, please read and reflect on Genesis 7:

1. In what ways, if any, has this chapter impacted your understanding of the Flood story?

2. Greg thinks the best evidence suggests that there was a local, not a global, flood that the Genesis Flood story is echoing. Yet he argues that the author of this narrative depicts the Flood as "the undoing of the entire creation." How are these two claims consistent, in Greg's mind? Do you agree or disagree with him?

Here are some additional study questions to help silently engage with Greg's thoughts:

1. Does the existence of something like *The Epic of Gilgamesh* (or the other ANE flood narratives) impact your understanding of the biblical account in any way? If so, how?

2. How is God's motivation in Genesis different from Enlil's motivation in *The Epic of Gilgamesh*?

3. Whether you personally embrace Greg's interpretation or not, list what he describes as the *direct* and *indirect* revelations of God's character in the Flood narrative? How does the portrait of God in the Flood narrative compare to the revelation of God in the crucified Christ?

Here are some questions to process as a group:

1. What aspects of this narrative would you consider *direct* revelations—viz. places in the narrative where you discern the Spirit breaking through to reveal things that are consistent with the character of God that is revealed in the crucified Christ? Conversely, what aspects of this narrative would you consider to be *indirect* revelations?

2. Greg says, "by singling out Noah as the one person who 'walked faithfully with God' ([Gen] 6:9), this author is suggesting that God was down to his last man! *This* is why Yahweh needed to go to the extreme of withdrawing his Spirit and allowing forces of destruction to revert creation back to a 'formless and void' state. So, while the Flood was a grievous judgment on the world, it was even more fundamentally *a rescue operation*. Only by going to this extreme could God preserve his dream for eventually uniting himself to humans and inviting them to share in his triune love and rule forever" (*CV* 202–3). Have you ever thought of the Flood narrative along those lines before? Does this change your perspective on this story in any way?

3. What remaining questions and/or objections do you have concerning the material covered in this chapter?

QUESTIONS AND ANSWERS: Here are some questions Greg has received on this material followed by his responses:

Q1: What would you say to skeptics who argue that there is no way a pair of every species of animal on the earth could travel to wherever Noah's ark was located, and no way for all these animals to fit onto, and to survive in, this ark for almost a year even if they all somehow managed to find their way to it?

A1: I'm inclined to agree with skeptics who argue alone these lines. So far as I can tell, the geological and archeological evidence seems to suggest that the biblical Flood narrative (as well as other ANE flood narratives) was likely based on a massive regional flood involving the Mediterranean and Black Seas that took place around 5600 BCE. For his own theological reasons, the biblical author interpreted this (or some other) flood as the undoing of the entire creation.

In any event, the question of how the Flood narrative relates to actual history is actually irrelevant to our interpretation of this narrative, for it is the narrative itself that is "God-breathed," regardless of how it relates to actual history.

Q2: If God was justified in allowing cosmic forces to undo creation because it was the only way to continue with his plan for humanity, why wouldn't God be justified reversing creation himself, as the author of this narrative claims?

A2: While one could argue God would be justified reversing creation and therefore bringing about the deaths of untold numbers of people, I am convinced Jesus's cross-centered life and ministry reveals a God who refuses to engage in such behavior. On top of this, the cross reveals that, while God's judgments often involve violence, it is agents other than God who always carry out this violence. And, finally, while the author of the Flood narrative clearly believes God sent the Flood, he nevertheless attributes all the violence to "the deep," understood as a destructive cosmic force.

Q3: Would you agree that the story of the "sons of God" having sex with the "daughters of men" to beget "Nephilim" (Gen 6:1–4) reads like it belongs to the genre of legend rather than to history? Moreover, if we interpreted this passage as history rather than legend, how could we possibly explain why Yahweh would allow such a thing to happen, since it almost resulted in derailing God's plans for humanity?

A3: Even if we concluded that this story belongs to the genre of legend, this wouldn't mean that we would be free to treat this story any less seriously than we treat historical passages, for all Scripture is God-breathed and deserves to be treated as such. Having said this, I don't believe the mere fact that a story talks about supernatural agents having sex with human women is itself sufficient grounds for declaring the story a legend. Sometimes reality is stranger than fiction.

Moreover, the fact that this author identifies the Nephilim as "the heroes . . . of old" and "warriors of renown" (6:4), whom he assumes his audience is already familiar with, reinforces the sense that the author is intending to pass on historical material.

As to why God would allow this, I would think it sufficient to appeal to the free will of "the sons of God." These rebel agents apparently had the God-given "say-so" to freely use their superior position to either aid humans or to exploit humans to their own advantage, and they unfortunately chose the latter. Moreover, human free will also played into this inasmuch as the narrative suggests that it was human corruption that opened the door to these agents and other forces of destruction to begin corrupting the entire creation.

RECOMMENDED RESOURCES: Greg recommends the following material that discusses various issues and perspectives on material covered in this chapter:

Anderson, B. *From Creation to New Creation: Old Testament Perspectives*. Minneapolis: Fortress Press, 1994.

Boyd, G. *The Crucifixion of the Warrior God: Interpreting the Old Testament's Violent Portraits of God in Light of the Cross*. 2 vols. Minneapolis: Fortress Press, 2017. 2:1098–142.

Clifford, R. J. *Creation Accounts in the Ancient Near East and in the Bible*. Washington, DC: Catholic Biblical Association of America, 1994.

Davis, D. A. *The Biblical Flood: A Case Study of the Church's Response to Extrabiblical Evidence*. Grand Rapids: Eerdmans, 1995.

Fretheim, T. F. *Creation Untamed: The Bible, God, and Natural Disasters*. Grand Rapids: Baker Academic, 2010.

———. *God and World in the Old Testament: A Relational Theology of Creation*. Nashville: Abingdon, 2005.

Heidel, A. *The Babylonian Genesis: The Story of Creation*. Chicago: University of Chicago Press, 1951.

———. *The Gilgamesh Epic and Old Testament Parallels*. Chicago: University of Chicago Press, 1949.

Kloos, C. *Yhwh's Combat with the Sea: A Canaanite Tradition in the Religion of Ancient Israel*. Leiden: Brill, 1986.

Wilson, I. *Before the Flood: The Biblical Flood as Real Event and How it Changed the Source of Civilization*. New York: St. Martin's, 2001.

van Wolde, E. *Stories of the Beginning: Genesis 1–11 and Other Creation Stories*. Translated by J. Bowden. London: SCM, 1996.

Youngblood, R., ed. *The Genesis Debate: Persistent Questions About Creation and Flood*. Grand Rapids: Baker, 1990.

Week #9: Part I— Dragon-Swallowing-Dragon Warfare: How God Wins

Everyone knows the ultimate goal of a military battle, or of most forms of competition, is to win. The apostle Paul himself encourages us to "run the race" of our lives in such a way as to "win the prize" (1 Cor 9:24). Regardless of how intense our own internal competitive streak runs, all of us want to win on one level or another. Whether it's about our own athletic endeavors or the teams we choose to root for, we want to experience "the thrill of victory" and avoid "the agony of defeat" as much as possible.

Living in Lawrence, Kansas, I am part of a community that takes huge pride in the winning tradition of its men's college basketball team. Not to brag (too much), but as of 2018 the Kansas Jayhawks have won fourteen straight regular season conference titles, the most of any team in history. Kansas University is one of the winningest programs in the United States, with three national championships and fifteen final-four appearances, and is second on the list of all time wins with over 2,200 victories in its storied history. Clearly, winning is a *big deal* here!

When it comes to winning, however, the question is: does it matter *how* you win? Given baseball fans' reaction to the news of rampant steroid use and its impact on historic records, or golfing fans' reaction when players fail to report themselves for a violation (or even worse, when they get caught cheating!), it's clear that, to most of us, the answer is: yes. How the victory is achieved *matters*.

This chapter explores this dynamic as we consider the victory of God over Egypt and Pharaoh as seen in the narratives covering Israel's exodus and the crossing of the Red Sea. We see not only *that* God wins but also explore *how* God wins. In the process, we'll also see how the cross-centered interpretation of this narrative reveals God's nonviolent character and Aikido way of defeating evil, which were supremely revealed in the crucified Christ.

THE BIG IDEA: God uses evil to conquer evil.

FINDING JESUS: "So, while the author of this narrative credits Yahweh with violence, the truth is that God was directly involved in none of it. Rather, from start to finish God fought and overcame evil in this battle using the same Aikido strategy he employed on the cross." (*CV* 215)

TERMS AND DEFINITIONS: Major concepts from this lesson include:

- *yam* = the Hebrew word for "sea" (*yam*) also happens to be the name of a well-known Canaanite deity associated with chaos; many OT scholars argue that many times in the OT when "*yam*" is used, it is referring to this mythological sea monster, not simply to H_2O

• *tannin* = the Hebrew word for "serpent" that can also be translated "dragon" or "monster"

REFERENCES AND REFLECTIONS

Here is a summary of Greg's main points from this chapter:

The Deliverance and Drowning at the Red Sea: "We need to remember that the people of this time and area considered heavenly and earthly battles to be two sides of the same reality. And . . . things like mighty seas and raging waters in the OT often do not merely refer to H_2O, for they were one of the primary ways ANE people envisioned the anti-creational cosmic forces that threaten the world." (*CV* 207)

A Victory over a Cosmic Beast: "[As we see in numerous OT passages,] Yahweh's victory [at the crossing of the Red Sea] wasn't first and foremost over Pharaoh's army, it was over the 'waters' and 'depths' that 'writhed' and 'convulsed' in fear as he approached [Psalm 77]. . . . By interpreting the parting of the Red Sea within a conflict-with-chaos framework . . . [we see how] Yahweh's historical victory over the Red Sea reenacts his primeval victory over his cosmic foe when he created the present world. . . . It was the sea monster [the Red Sea], not God, who devoured Pharaoh's army. . . . Just as Yahweh restrained Pharaoh's army with a pillar of fire and then removed it to allow Pharaoh to do what he wanted to do, so too God restrained the cosmic monster to allow his people to march to safety, only then to remove his restraint, allowing this monster that was 'bent on destruction' to do what it wanted to do: namely, swallow people up (Exod 15:12)." (*CV* 209–10)

The Aikido Dimension of Yahweh's Victory—Part 1: "First, we saw in chapter 8 that biblical authors sometime viewed Pharaoh and/or Egypt as an anti-creational monster, the same way they identify the Red Sea with an anti-creational cosmic monster. . . . [T]his means that, from the biblical perspective, Yahweh was allowing one cosmic monster to swallow another." (*CV* 211–12)

The Aikido Dimension of Yahweh's Victory—Part 2: "This narrative, which culminates with God using one serpent (the Red Sea) to swallow another (Pharaoh and his army), began with God using Aaron's supernatural serpent to swallow Pharaoh's supernatural serpents (Exodus 7:8–13). . . . [T]he word for 'serpent' (*tannin*) in Exodus 7:12 does not refer to an ordinary snake. It could be translated as 'dragon' or 'monster,' and it happens to be the word that describes the anti-creational monster that Yahweh split asunder to save his people and overthrow the Egyptian army at the Red Sea (Ps 74:13; Isa 51:9). When we combine these considerations with the fact that Pharaoh and Egypt were themselves identified as an anti-creational monster, it's apparent that Yahweh's battle with Pharaoh begins and culminates with God 'using a dragon to swallow up a dragon.' As he did on the cross, God used evil to vanquish evil. . . . So while the author of the Exodus narrative believes he is exalting Yahweh by attributing the violence involved in each plague to him, these passages [Exod 12:23, Ps 78:49, Hab 3:5] provide further confirmation that Yahweh merely permitted a band of cosmic agents that were already bent on destruction to do what they wanted to do. And the one on which they are allowed to carry out their violence is Egypt, itself identified as a cosmic monster. It's apparent that, from beginning to end, God's judgment of Pharaoh and Egypt did not require God to act violently. He rather merely allowed one evil serpent to swallow another." (*CV* 212–14)

Battling the Gods of Egypt: "A compelling case can be made that each of the ten plagues was actually an assault on one or more of these Egyptian gods [Exod 12:23]. . . . [I]t seems that prior to God allowing one cosmic serpent (the Red Sea) to swallow another (Egypt, Pharaoh), God had already allowed one band of destroying angels (the agents behind the ten plagues) to swallow up another band of evil agents (the ten chief gods of Egypt) and to begin to undo creation in the land of Egypt. And this is why God's battle against Egypt and the Pharaoh, understood as yet another cosmic beast, is launched and is culminated with dragon-swallowing-dragon events. . . . Hence, while the surface meaning of the violent warrior portraits of God in this narrative contradict the revelation of God in the crucified Christ, the Aikido way that God used evil to vanquish evil is perfectly consistent with this revelation." (*CV* 215)

As you consider Greg's thoughts, please read and reflect on Exodus 14 and 15:

1. Has the idea of crediting God with the death of Pharaoh and his army ever seemed problematic to you in the past? Does it now? Why or why not?

2. What aspects of this story would you consider *direct* revelations, that is, places in the narrative where you discern the Spirit breaking through to reveal things that are consistent with the character of God that is revealed in the crucified Christ? Conversely, what aspects of this story would you consider to be *indirect* revelations?

Here are some additional study questions to help silently engage with Greg's thoughts:

1. Do you agree with Greg that our grasp of what "actually happened" in these biblical stories doesn't ultimately matter when it comes to our theological understanding of the text? Why or why not?

2. How does the information Greg provides on the plagues representing (or referring to) various Egyptian gods impact your understanding of this narrative?

Here are some questions to process as a group:

1. Describe the "dragon-swallowing-dragon" bookends to the exodus narrative. Which "dragons" swallow each other at the beginning, and which ones do so at the end?

2. Do you think Greg succeeded in demonstrating that God's Aikido way of responding to evil runs throughout the exodus narrative? If you think he succeeded, how does this affect how you understand this narrative?

3. Do you agree with Greg's claim that when God sees he must allow people to come under a judgment, he suffers much more than do the people being judged? How does this reinforce the cruciform interpretation of this passage?

4. What remaining questions and/or objections do you have concerning the material covered in this chapter?

QUESTIONS AND ANSWERS: Here are some questions Greg has received on this material followed by his responses:

Q1: The cruciform interpretation of the exodus and the drowning of Pharaoh's army in the Red Sea involves different groups of evil agents fighting against one another. But how do you reconcile this with Jesus's teaching that Satan's kingdom can't be divided against itself (Matt 12:25–27)?

A1: Jesus's teaching was meant only to refute the Pharisees' suggestion that he was casting out demons by the power of Satan. His response merely exposes the impossibility of Satan, the ruler of the kingdom of darkness, working at cross-purposes with himself by routing his own demonic troops. It does not rule out the possibility that various factions within Satan's empire could come into conflict with each other. In fact, if we consider for a moment the nature of evil, it seems to me that internal conflicts within the kingdom of darkness should be expected. So far as we are told, the agents comprising this kingdom lack any capacity for other-oriented love. These agents could therefore only be motivated by their own self-interest. This means that the only thing that could keep this domain from degenerating into chaos would be fear of its chief ruler, Satan. And since Satan is not omnipotent or omniscient, I submit that it would not be surprising if it turned out he was not always up to the task of enforcing his imposed unity.

But there is an alternative way of conceiving of how Yahweh might have used one group of spirit-agents to overthrow another. We have some biblical warrant for suspecting that the traditional view that all angelic beings are either all good or all evil is overly simplistic. Psalm 82 indicates that there are some "gods" that belong to the divine council but who are not yet unambiguously solidified in their allegiance or opposition to God. These "gods" had not been carrying out their assigned duty to "defend the weak and the fatherless" and to "uphold the cause of the poor and the oppressed" (Ps 82:3). Yahweh thus warned them that they will die "like mere mortals" if they do not amend their ways (Ps 82:7).

These "gods" are clearly not altogether evil, for they are members of God's heavenly council, but they are clearly also not altogether good, since they are disobeying God's commands to help the weak, the fatherless, the poor, and the oppressed. They are rather in a probationary stage where their fate has yet to be determined. In this light, we might suppose the "band of destroying angels" that God "unleashed" to defeat the "gods of Egypt" (Exod 12:12) belonged to this class of gods.

In this case, we could imagine God stooping to allow these imperfect cosmic agents to overthrow the gods of Egypt the same way God stoops to use sword-wielding governments to punish wrongdoers and to thereby keep sin in check (Rom 13:1–7). It's not that God approves of their sword wielding, but given that governments are going to wield swords, God will influence them as much as possible to carry out justice and punish wrongdoers.

Whichever one of these scenarios we decide is most plausible, they reconcile God's Aikido-like use of fallen (or at least imperfect) spirit-agents with Jesus's teaching about the impossibility of demons being cast out by the power of Satan.

Q2: In the exodus narrative, Pharaoh only changed his mind about letting the children of Israel go and to set out in pursuit of them because God had hardened his heart (Exod 14:4, 8, 17). God is depicted as hardening Pharaoh's heart at other points in the narrative as well. It thus looks like God is causing Pharaoh to sin and to doom his army to being drowned in the Red Sea. Since this is obviously a depiction of God that is radically inconsistent with what we learn about God's character in the crucified Christ, should we assume these passages reflect God humbly stooping to accommodate the fallen and culturally conditioned perspective of the author?

A2: We certainly could interpret this author's depiction of God hardening Pharaoh's heart to be a divine accommodation. But we shouldn't assume this to be the case too quickly. In keeping with the conservative hermeneutical principle, we should first explore exegetical ways of removing the difficulty this narrative presents. Only if there proves to be no adequate exegetical explanation should we accept these passages are divine accommodations. In the case of God hardening Pharaoh's heart, I'm inclined to think two exegetical considerations suffice.

First, it's significant that Pharaoh is said to have hardened his own heart five times, in response to the first five plagues, before Yahweh is portrayed as hardening his heart after the sixth plague. On this basis, one could argue that God's hardening of Pharaoh's heart did not cause Pharaoh to sin but was rather done in response to Pharaoh's sin.

Second, the particular form of the Hebrew word "to harden" (*chazaq*) that is used when Pharaoh is said to have hardened his own heart has the connotation of resisting something. When God is depicted as hardening Pharaoh's heart, however, a different form of the word is used, and it has the connotation of strengthening something. In this light, one could argue that once Yahweh saw there was no point trying to get Pharaoh to soften his heart toward him and repent, he decided to weave Pharaoh's hardness of heart into his sovereign plan by actually helping Pharaoh do what he really wanted to do, thereby allowing his hardness of heart to run its full self-destructive course. This may only imply that Yahweh buttressed Pharaoh's courage or that Yahweh's repeated attempts at persuading Pharaoh caused Pharaoh to become increasingly resolved in his stance against him.

Personally, I'm inclined to think these exegetical considerations suffice, which is why I can interpret these passages to be direct revelations. But should someone deem these explanations insufficient, they should interpret these passages to reflect divine accommodations and to therefore constitute indirect revelations.

RECOMMENDED RESOURCES: Greg recommends the following material that discusses various issues and perspectives on material covered in this chapter:

Batto, B. *Slaying the Dragon: Mythmaking in the Biblical Tradition.* Louisville: Westminster John Knox, 1992.

Boyd, G. *The Crucifixion of the Warrior God: Interpreting the Old Testament's Violent Portraits of God in Light of the Cross.* 2 vols. Minneapolis: Fortress Press, 2017. 2:1143–92.

Day, J. *God's Conflict with the Dragon and the Sea: Echoes of a Canaanite Myth in the Old Testament.* New York: Cambridge University Press, 1985.

Fretheim, T. F. *God and World in the Old Testament: A Relational Theology of Creation.* Nashville: Abingdon, 2005.

———. "The Plagues as Ecological Signs of Historical Disaster." *Journal of Biblical Literature* 110, no. 3 (1991): 385–87.

Kloos, C. *Yhwh's Combat with the Sea: A Canaanite Tradition in the Religion of Ancient Israel.* Leiden: Brill, 1986.

Lind, M. *Yahweh Is a Warrior: The Theology of Warfare in Israel.* Scottdale, PA: Herald, 1980.

Miller, P. D. *The Divine Warrior in Ancient Israel.* Cambridge, MA: Harvard University Press, 1973.

van der Toorn, K., B Becking, and P. W. van der Horst. *Dictionary of Deities and Demons in the Bible.* 2nd ed. Grand Rapids: Eerdmans, 1999.

Week #9: Part II—Misusing Divine Power: Those Temperamental Prophets

Some lessons just stick with you. While the majority of college lectures and Sunday sermons I've listened to over the years have (for the most part) escaped my memory, there are some I remember as if they happened yesterday. One such memory concerns a former Old Testament theology professor from my undergrad years walking us through the book of Judges. I especially recall his comments on Samson and how he forever transformed my mental image of this biblical character, describing him as "The Original Dumb Jock."

With all due apology to the athletes out there who understandably bristle at this admittedly harsh stereotype, I still laugh when I think of that label and just how appropriate it is, despite how different it was from anything I had ever heard. In all the sermons or Sunday-school lessons I had heard before, the only thing that was emphasized about Samson was his long hair, his incredible strength, and—if the teacher was feeling like really pushing the envelope—his weakness for "the ladies."

Similarly, the only thing I ever remember being taught about Elijah and Elisha were how awesome they were and how God mightily worked through them to accomplish his will. Perhaps your experience was different, but not once, in any of these instances, do I recall questions being raised about the morality of these men's supernatural exploits. Nor did I invest any time considering their stories from the perspective of those they had killed in the process.

This chapter remedied that, however, and I'm grateful for it. As with the previous narratives we've considered, it's good to wrestle with these stories and get clarity on who is responsible for what in the midst of the details, especially when our view of God's moral character is on the line. For we are seeking to consistently see him as the same God revealed through the crucified Christ, and that's what this chapter helps us do.

THE BIG IDEA: The supernatural authority God gives to certain individuals is subject to their own will and can thus be used in ways God does not approve of.

FINDING JESUS: "We must see the cross, understood as the thematic center of everything Jesus was about, as the quintessential witness to God's willingness to entrust divine authority to humans as well as the supreme illustration of the proper use of this divine authority." (*CV* 221)

TERMS AND DEFINITIONS: Major concepts from this lesson include:

  • **free will** = the limited amount of "say-so" God grants to every human being, which God refuses to coercively override for his own purposes

- *paradidōmi* = the Greek word for "committed" or "entrusted"; in this case, how God entrusted divine authority to Jesus's fully human will as part of his incarnation

REFERENCES AND REFLECTIONS

Here is a summary of Greg's main points from this chapter:

Introduction: "When exceptional authority is given to someone, there's no guarantee that they will use it the way they should." (*CV* 218)

Misusing Divine Power: "Just because a person has received exceptional authority from God does not mean that the way they use it agrees with God. . . . When certain people whom God has entrusted with supernatural authority bring about supernaturally caused violence, the looking-glass cross allows us to discern that the responsibility for this violence falls on the agent who had been entrusted with this power, not on the God who entrusted the agent with it." (*CV* 221–22)

Calling Down Fire from Heaven: "There are several considerations that confirm that this killing was not God's will. . . . Jesus would not have approved of Elijah's violent and self-protective use of divine authority had he used it this way during Jesus's ministry. . . . Elijah's self-protective display of supernatural violence was contrary to the Lord's will . . . [and his] fear-motivated misuse of divine authority was predicated on a sinful lack of trust in Yahweh." (*CV* 222–23)

Elisha and the Mauling Bears: "For one thing, while Elisha cursed these boys 'in the name of the Lord' (2 Kgs 2:24), the text does not claim that Yahweh sent the bears. . . . Whether it's legendary or historical in nature, the narrative of Elisha's lethal curse is not intended to hold him up as a model of exemplary behavior. . . . Moreover, in the OT and the broader ANE culture, demonic forces were frequently associated with wild beasts in the desert. In this light, we should probably interpret the two mauling bears in this narrative to represent forces of evil that were unleashed by Elisha's protection-removing curse. . . . This story shows Elisha using the authority he had been given to defend himself by *sacrificing others*. At the same time, . . . [this narrative] also bears witness to the truth that the one who perfectly submitted his divine authority to the Father also bore the sin of all those who, like Elisha, did not." (*CV* 226–27)

The Supernatural Strength of a Long-Haired Brawler: "Samson acquired supernatural strength when the Spirit of the Lord came upon him and/or when his hair grew long [Judg 14:6, 19; 15:4; 16:22]. But Samson consistently used this strength in remarkably selfish, vengeful, violent, and often foolish ways. . . . When we read the stories of Samson . . . we can only marvel at the humility of God who, out of covenantal love for his people, would stoop to work through legends of a man as infantile and degenerate as Samson. . . . [A]t no point does the author show Samson seeking God's will about the use of this supernatural strength. Nor does the author ever depict Samson aspiring to use this power for the glory of God. Samson rather uses the divine power that was entrusted to him for personal gain and personal retaliation. . . . Samson's use of God-given power tells us nothing about God's true character." (*CV* 227–30)

Conclusion: "God would rather have a risky creation in which free agents are capable of genuine love than a risk-free creation in which agents are not truly free. . . . God has always been willing to endow certain individuals with even more agency by giving them a degree of his own power. And God has always done this knowing that, because these agents are free, there's no guarantee that they will always use this power the way he desires." (*CV* 230)

As you consider Greg's thoughts, please read and reflect on Luke 9:51–56:

1. As Orthodox Jews, James and John (who Jesus interestingly nicknames the "sons of thunder" in Mark 3) would have been familiar with the story of Elijah. Based on Luke's account, what do James and John's request to call down fire from heaven tells us about how they interpreted Elijah's actions and about their views on the use of violence?

2. How is Jesus's response to James and John consistent with what Jesus teaches elsewhere?

Here are some additional study questions to help silently engage with Greg's thoughts:

1. As Elijah, Elisha, and Samson exercise their own "free will" in ways that don't honor God, do their actions indict the character of God, or their own character?

2. Have you ever thought of these men as acting against God's will in these instances? Has Greg's account of these OT characters changed the way you think about them? Why or why not?

3. Is there any way you can see Jesus supporting the violent actions of Elijah, Elisha, and Samson? Why or why not?

Here are some questions to process as a group:

1. Read 1 Corinthians 14:32. How do Paul's instructions about maintaining a sense of order in worship relate to the thesis Greg is advocating in this chapter?

2. Do you believe God is ultimately culpable for Elijah, Elisha, and Samson's actions since he entrusted supernatural authority to them? Or do you think these men are responsible for their own actions?

3. What are some other analogies from day-to-day life that illustrate this concept in ways we can directly relate to? (E.g., a parent entrusting the car keys to their child.)

4. How might the concept of divine power being submitted to human wills help explain the deaths of Ananias and Sapphira in Acts 5:1–11?

5. What remaining questions and/or objections do you have concerning any of the material covered in this chapter?

QUESTIONS AND ANSWERS: Here are some questions Greg has received on this material followed by his responses:

Q1: Why didn't God just revoke the supernatural authority he'd given to people when he saw that they were going to misuse it? Doesn't the very fact that God didn't stop Elijah and others from using their supernatural authority in violent ways suggest that this use was not contrary to God's will?

A1: Since the supernatural authority that God gives to certain individuals is subject to the free will of the individuals God gives it to, we should think of this authority as an augmentation of these individuals' free will. And if we think through the implications of this, it means that this supernatural authority is *irrevocable*.

Free will is the God-given ability to choose to go *this* way to such and such an extent, or *that* way to such and such an extent. Now, if God were to revoke your ability to go *that* way because he didn't approve of it, then God obviously *didn't* give you the ability to go this way *or that way* to such and such an extent. By definition, if God truly gives you the ability to choose to go this *or that way*, God cannot revoke your ability to choose to go *that* way. God cannot revoke free will, whether it's endowed with supernatural authority or not, for the same reason God cannot create a round triangle or a married bachelor.

So, once God decided to place a degree of supernatural authority under the free will of certain individuals, he could not revoke it simply because he saw that it was about to be misused.

Q2: In Hebrews 11:32–34, the author praises the faith of "Gideon, Barak, Samson, Jephthah . . . David and Samuel and the prophets" who "through faith conquered kingdoms . . . became mighty in war" and "put foreign armies to flight." If God is altogether opposed to violence, how can this author praise the faith of these OT heroes when this faith led them to engage in violence?

A2: The fact that this author praises the faith of an OT hero does not imply that they endorse every aspect of this hero's life or the way this hero lived out their faith. For example, this author praises the faith of Rahab without mentioning her being a prostitute. But I seriously doubt anyone would conclude from this that this author condoned her profession.

Similarly, this author praises the faith of Gideon, but must we on this basis conclude that they condoned all of Gideon's grotesquely violent exploits, including skinning alive all the elders of Succoth with thorns and briers just because they had taunted him (Judg 8:18)?

This author also praises the faith of Samson, but as we saw in this chapter, Samson's life was anything but morally praiseworthy. Are we to believe the author of Hebrews condoned Samson murdering thirty random civilians just so he could get their clothes and pay off a debt he foolishly incurred (Judg 3:19)?

Along the same lines, this author praises the faith of Jephthah, even though Jephthah expressed this faith by sacrificing his only daughter as "a burnt offering" to the Lord in exchange for a military victory (Judg 8:29–40).

The point is, it is possible to extoll the power of a person's faith as well as other virtuous aspects of their character without thereby condoning all the ways they express their faith and character. The author of Hebrews is praising the *power of faith* that allowed some to "conquer kingdoms" and "put armies to flight," but this doesn't mean he assumed that their military exploits were godly.

Q3: The apostle Paul clearly understood the full revelation of God in the crucified Christ, yet he once used the supernatural authority he'd been given to blind a magician named Elymas (Acts 13:9–12). Blinding someone is a violent act. So, if Paul's violent use of supernatural power doesn't contradict the revelation of God in the crucified Christ, why should we conclude that the OT characters that used supernatural power in violent ways is inconsistent with this revelation?

A3: The fact that the early church had received the full revelation of God in the crucified Christ doesn't mean that everyone in the early church fully understood or consistently lived out the implications of this revelation. If we had to, therefore, we could argue that Paul was frustrated by Elymas's interference with his missionary work and thus misused the supernatural authority he'd been given when he blinded him. But I don't believe we need to go this route, for I don't see anything inherently unloving about Paul's action here.

Paul only temporarily blinded Elymas, and he did this because Elymas was trying to prevent the proconsul of Cyprus from embracing Christ. And, interestingly enough, this display of supernatural power so impressed this proconsul that he became a Christian on the spot. It thus seems that Paul temporarily afflicted Elymas in the loving hope that both Elymas and the proconsul would come to see the light (pun intended) and embrace faith in Christ.

We can perhaps think of Paul's action in this episode along the lines of a surgeon who must break a patient's badly cracked bone so it will eventually heal correctly or who must cut a patient open to repair their damaged heart and save their life. In any other context, breaking someone's leg or cutting a person open would constitute violent acts. When done by a doctor to benefit a patient, however, these are clearly loving actions. So too, while Paul's action would constitute violence if it was done with the intention of harming Elymas, the fact that it was done with the hope of saving both Elymas and the proconsul makes it loving.

Could one argue along these lines for the violent exploits of Elijah, Elisha, and Samson or for all of the portraits of God commanding and engaging in violence? Well, one could *try*. In fact, this was precisely what I intended to argue when I set out to write a book on this topic in 2007. After completing about fifty pages, however, I decided I had to abandon the project. I found that even my best arguments were utterly unconvincing.

While it's not at all hard to imagine the loving motive that led Paul to temporarily afflict Elymas, what possible loving motive can we imagine God having for commanding his people to mercilessly slaughter entire populations of children and infants, and to do so as an act of worship to him? Or what loving motive can we attribute to Samson when he murdered thirty random civilians to steal their clothes to pay off a debt he had foolishly incurred? I had to admit I could find none, and this is what forced me to consider a completely different approach to interpreting these episodes. The result, eleven years later, is the book you are now reading.

RECOMMENDED RESOURCES: Greg recommends the following material that discusses various issues and perspectives on material covered in this chapter:

Boyd, G. *Crucifixion of the Warrior God: Interpreting the Old Testament's Violent Portraits of God in Light of the Cross*, 2 vols. Minneapolis: Fortress Press, 2017. 2:1195–247.

Fretheim, T. F. "Issues of Agency in Exodus." In *The Book of Exodus: Composition, Reception and Interpretation*, edited by T. B. Dozeman, C. A. Evans, and J. N. Lohr, 591–609. Boston: Brill, 2014.

———. *The Suffering of God: An Old Testament Perspective*. Philadelphia: Fortress Press, 1984.

Hays, R. *The Faith of Jesus Christ: The Narrative Substructure of Galatians 3:1–4:11*. Grand Rapids: Eerdmans, 2002.

Johnson, A. R. *The One and the Many in the Israelite Conception of God*. Cardiff: University of Wales Press, 1961.

Kitz, A. M. *Cursed Are You! The Phenomenology of Cursing in Cuneiform and Hebrew Texts*. Winona Lake, IL: Eisenbrauns, 2014.

McDonald, P. *God and Violence: Biblical Recourses for Living in a Small World*. Scottdale, PA: Herald, 2004.

Sommer, B. D. *The Bodies of God and the World of Ancient Israel*. Cambridge, MA: Harvard University Press, 2009.

Week #10: Part I—Commanding Child Sacrifice: Trusting God in the Midst of Confusion

The story of Abraham sacrificing Isaac is a deeply challenging one for all of us, whether we have our own children or not. For me and my wife, Jill, it seems especially poignant as we only have one child: a young boy named—you guessed it—Isaac, who is probably a few years younger than Abraham and Sarah's son was at the time this story took place.

Like many other couples (and perhaps like some of you participating in this study), we were unable to have biological children despite trying to do so for over ten years. After years of prayerful tears, however, we were so grateful to become Isaac's adoptive parents just six weeks after his birth. I can still recall the first time I held him in my arms so many years ago, how soft his little hands were, how mesmerizing his little head smelled (which is when I discovered the famed "baby smell" really is a thing!).

Having loved him and cared for him these many years, I absolutely cannot imagine the emotional anguish I would experience if *any-*

one—much less *God*—asked me to give him up for any reason, to say nothing of asking me to *sacrifice* him. Thankfully, I am absolutely confident God would *never* ask me to do such a thing. Why? Because having seen the full revelation of God in the crucified Christ, I am absolutely confident in God's good and loving character. I don't know God *fully*, of course, but I know God *enough* to trust that this kind of request will never be asked of me.

But here's the thing: Abraham didn't have the same understanding of God's character that we're privileged to have this side of the cross. On top of that, he grew up in an environment where sacrificing children to prove one's loyalty to a particular god was common. With all that in mind, it's hard for us to imagine what Abraham, Sarah, and Isaac were going through in this narrative, though this chapter tries to help us imagine just that.

THE BIG IDEA: God is not like the ANE gods who demanded child sacrifice.

FINDING JESUS: "Abraham . . . named the place where he had bound Isaac, 'The Lord will provide' [Genesis 22:14]. And those of us who know God as he is fully revealed in the crucified Christ know more deeply than Abraham possibly could the profundity of this name. For on Calvary we learn that, rather than requiring humans to offer up sacrifices to him, the true God sacrifices himself for all humans." (*CV* 242-43)

TERMS AND DEFINITIONS: Major concepts from this lesson include:

• **Conservative Hermeneutical Principle** (a reminder from *Building on Tradition*) = the decision to interpret any given passage of Scripture in a way that sticks as faithfully as possible to its originally intended meaning

• **paradigm shift** = a fundamental change in approach or underlying assumptions; an important change that happens when the usual way of thinking about something is replaced by a new and different way

REFERENCES AND REFLECTIONS

Here is a summary of Greg's main points from this chapter:

The Cross-Centered Interpretation: "If the interpretation I am about to propose is deemed compelling, it means the portrait of God contained in this narrative can be interpreted as a *direct* rather than an *indirect* revelation of the God who is fully revealed in the crucified Christ. . . . Abraham's testing illustrates the challenge that we've been wrestling with throughout this book, namely: What should you do when you are convinced God is loving and faithful but then seem to find him apparently acting in unloving and unfaithful ways?" (*CV* 234)

Challenges to Copan's Interpretation: "[I am arguing that] Yahweh stooped to momentarily take on the appearance of a typical ANE child-sacrifice-demanding deity by giving this horrific command. I'm suggesting Yahweh didn't merely stoop to *allow* Abraham or others *to believe* he gave this command. In this one instance, the heavenly missionary stooped to *actually* *give it!* And Yahweh did this to have Abraham undergo a highly emotional paradigm shift in his view of God that removed any doubt that Yahweh might be like other ANE gods who required this ultimate sacrifice. Indeed, far from demanding sacrifice, Abraham needed to learn that Yahweh is a God who makes sacrifices." (*CV* 236)

A Curious Compliance: "Yahweh's command to sacrifice Isaac simply didn't shock Abraham the way the announced plan to have Sodom and Gomorrah destroyed did. . . . [T]he revelation that Yahweh was actually revolted by child sacrifices was not given until the Sinai covenant, which took place hundreds of years later. . . . [W]e have no account of Yahweh explicitly telling Abraham that he was not like other ANE gods when it came to demanding child sacrifices. . . . While God wanted to determine Abraham's level of obedience and trust, he even more importantly wanted to remove any lingering suspicion Abraham had that Yahweh might have a side to him that was like the child-devouring gods he had previously worshipped." (*CV* 237–38)

The Instructional Strategy of Pushing to the Edge: "Given their pagan past, . . . [Abraham and Sarah's ploy with Hagar in Genesis 16:4] is almost to be expected, for a uniform aspect of the common theology of the ANE was that deities need humans to do their part in order to receive divine blessings. The long delay in receiving the son that Yahweh had promised apparently led these former pagans to conclude that Yahweh needed their help in delivering on his promise. . . . Yet, even after this contrived plan failed, Yahweh waited another thirteen years before delivering on his promise! Why? It seems Yahweh was taking this couple 'to the edge,' where they could easily despair of ever receiving their promised son, as a means of freeing them from every last vestige of their pagan assumption that God needed their help. . . . Yahweh had to bring Abraham and Sarah to a point where it looked as though Yahweh was not going to fulfill his promise . . . in order to convince them that . . . Yahweh is able to fulfill his promises without any human help whatsoever." (*CV* 238–40)

Pushing Abraham to the Edge: "Sacrificing one's firstborn child was the ultimate 'work' a human could perform to prove their loyalty to a god or to court a god's favor. So if there remained any suspicion that Yahweh was in any respect like other ANE gods, it would be about this. . . . God was once again stooping to meet his covenant partner where he was at in order to lead him to where he wanted him to be. . . . Out of love for Abraham and a desire to see him set free of his lingering pagan conceptions of him, Yahweh in this one instance *actually* stooped to play this role. . . . God once again pushed Abraham to the edge for the purpose of dramatically reframing his conception of him. . . . Through this testing, Abraham demonstrated the same level of loyalty that the pagan gods demand when they required a child sacrifice. But this dramatic paradigm shift enabled Abraham to understand that his ultimate loyalty was to a God who not only did not *require* child sacrifice, he *provides* the sacrifice." (*CV* 240–42)

As you consider Greg's thoughts, please read and reflect on Genesis 22:1–14:

1. The author of Genesis said, "God tested Abraham" (v.1). According to Greg's interpretation, what was the nature of that test really about?

2. In light of Greg's interpretive proposal, how would this process have shifted Abraham's perspective of God's character? How would that character have been different from the other pagan gods?

Here are some additional study questions to help silently engage with Greg's thoughts:

1. What are Greg's two main concerns with Paul Copan's perspective on this story?

2. Which reading is more compelling to you: Copan's or Greg's? Why?

Here are some questions to process as a group:

1. It seems like God could have simply said, "Hey Abraham, you know that child sacrifice thing? Don't do that," and that could have been the end of it. But what indication do we have from the broader testimony of Scripture that such a strategy would not have worked?

2. Of all the cruciform interpretations we've walked through so far (the Flood, the exodus, Korah's rebellion, the crossing of the Red Sea, the temperamental prophets, the testing of Abraham), which one is the most difficult for you to come to terms with? Why?

3. Greg writes, "Unless we fully trust the revelation of God in the crucified Christ . . . we will not have the motivation or the capacity to discern how these ugly violent portraits bear witness to the unsurpassable beauty of God revealed in the crucified Christ" (*CV* 244). Having come this far in the study, has your mental image of God's character changed in any way? Do you feel like you have a better understanding of how the violent portraits of God serve to point us to the crucified Christ? How would you put that in your own words?

4. What remaining questions and/or objections do you have concerning the material covered in this chapter?

QUESTIONS AND ANSWERS: Here are some questions Greg has received on this material followed by his responses:

Q1: I understand why God needed to push Abraham "to the edge," but what about poor Isaac? Coming within a moment of being bludgeoned by your own father must have been emotionally scarring for this young man. Was it loving for God to put him through that?

A1: It would certainly be traumatizing for a contemporary Western young man to be subjected to this sort of treatment, but it is anachronistic to project our modern sensibilities onto people in ancient cultures. We of course can't know exactly what Isaac was thinking and feeling as his father bound him and placed him over the wood, as though he was about to sacrifice him. Perhaps Isaac trusted to the very end his father's promise that "God himself will provide the lamb for a burnt offering" (Gen 22:8). But even if Isaac suspected his father was going to sacrifice him, one thing is certain: in the ANE, where child sacrifices were common, the prospect of being sacrificed by his father wouldn't have shocked Isaac the way it would shock any contemporary young man. In fact, in many ancient cultures it was considered a high honor to be chosen to be a offered up as a sacrifice to a god, for it was believed that this heroic sacrifice ensured the safety and well-being of one's family, tribe, and/or nation.

In any event, as we follow Isaac's story in the Bible following the event on Mount Moriah, there is no indication that this event had a lasting negative effect on him. And given the prevalence of child sacrifice throughout the ANE, this is not at all surprising.

Q2: If you grant that in this one instance Yahweh stooped to take on the appearance of a rather typical ANE god by actually commanding Abraham to sacrifice Isaac, why do you insist that in every other instance Yahweh merely stooped to allow his people to mistakenly think he commanded his people to engage in violence? In other words, might God have stooped to appear as an ANE deity by actually commanding his people to show no mercy and to slaughter entire populations in the land of Canaan?

A2: In keeping with my commitment to the Conservative Hermeneutical Principle, I believe we must stick as close as possible to the surface meaning of passages and only look for "something else going on" when the surface meaning of a passage conflicts with what we learn about God in Jesus's cross-centered life and ministry. I find nothing in the surface meaning of the story of Abraham being commanded to offer up Isaac that conflicts with this revelation when it is framed along the lines of shock therapy, as I argued in this chapter. By contrast, I find no way of sticking to the surface meaning of the OT's other violent portraits of God that doesn't contradict the revelation of God in the crucified Christ.

It's one thing if God, with a loving motive, sought to free Abraham from his residual paganism by temporarily playing the role of an ANE deity who demands a child sacrifice, and to not follow through with this command. It's something very different, however, if God, with no discernable loving motive, were to stoop to play the role of an ANE deity who commands merciless genocide and to let his people follow through with this command. The first set a hero of the faith free to understand God more accurately; the second resulted in untold numbers of men, women, children, infants and animals being ruthlessly sacrificed to him. The first is consistent with Jesus's cross-centered life and ministry, while the second is not.

RECOMMENDED RESOURCES: Greg recommends the following material that discusses various issues and perspectives on material covered in this chapter:

Bergmann, M., M. J. Murray, and M. C. Rea, eds. *Divine Evil? The Moral Character of the God of Abraham*. New York: Oxford University Press, 2013.

Boyd, G. *The Crucifixion of the Warrior God: Interpreting the Old Testament's Violent Portraits of God in Light of the Cross*. 2 vols. Minneapolis: Fortress Press, 2017. 2:1283–96.

Fretheim, T. *Abraham, Trials of Family and Faith*. Columbia: University of South Carolina Press, 2007.

Gibson, T. *A God Named Desire*. Nampa, ID: Pacific Press, 2010.

Thompson, A. *Who's Afraid of the Old Testament God?* 4th ed. Gonzalez, FL: Pacesetters Bible School, 2003.

Week #10: Part II—Four Words of Encouragement

As we come to the end of our study, let's consider the closing words of encouragement from *Cross Vision.*

THE BIG IDEA: "The depth of your passion for God and of your transformation into his likeness will never outrun the beauty of your mental representation of God." (*CV* 248)

FINDING JESUS: "God *really is* as beautiful as the cross reveals him to be!" (*CV* 247)

FINAL WORDS OF ENCOURAGEMENT

Maintain Full Confidence of Christ's Revelation of God's Character: "First, remember that the cross only functions as a looking-glass that enables us to discern *what else is going on* behind the scenes of the OT's violent portraits when we remain fully confident that Jesus's cross-centered life and ministry fully reveal what God is like." (*CV* 248)

God Is More Beautiful Than You Can Possibly Imagine:
"Second, if you were once accustomed to believing in a God
who has a dark side, you will likely sometimes find yourself
thinking that allowing the cross to completely define your conception of God *feels too good to be true*. If that happens, embrace it
as good news! For the truth is that, however beautiful you envision God, he is infinitely *more* beautiful than that!" (*CV* 249)

In Literary Crucifixes, Ugliness Reflects the Ugliness of Sin:
"Third, when you come across ugly portraits of God in the
Bible, remind yourself that this ugliness is a reflection of the
ugliness of our sin that Jesus bore on the cross." (*CV* 249)

The Spirit and the Sanctified Imagination: "Finally . . . invest
a good amount of time cultivating an ever-deepening relationship with the God of self-sacrificial love revealed on Calvary. . . .
[I]n Christ, God has given us a vivid, concrete, flawless expression of exactly what he is like. . . . [A]sk the Spirit to help you
vividly imagine the beautiful, true God revealed in Christ, and
especially in Christ crucified. . . . [R]egularly take time to surrender your imagination to the Spirit, asking him to help you see
God's perfect, infinitely intense love for you in the eyes of Jesus.
. . . [T]he more vivid and real you experience the crucified God,
the more *unreal* the violent portraits of God that conflict with
this vision will feel. And the more unreal these portraits feel,
the more naturally you will interpret them through the looking-
glass cross." (*CV* 249–50)

QUESTIONS TO PROCESS IN COMMUNITY: Here there are
no prescribed questions. Just open it up for questions, discussions,
observations, and a time of closing prayer.

QUESTIONS AND ANSWERS: Here are some questions Greg has received on this material, and his responses:

Q1: You stress the importance of using your imagination to experience Jesus, but I have always heard that the use of the imagination to enhance spiritual experiences is a part of the "New Age Movement."

A1: In 2 Corinthians 3, Paul draws an analogy between the veil that concealed the glory of God that shined through Moses's face, on the one hand, and the veil that is over the minds of unbelievers, on the other (vv. 13–15). "When one turns to the Lord," however, Paul says "the veil is removed" (v. 16) and the Spirit sets us free to see Jesus (v. 17). And so, Paul continues, "all of us, with unveiled faces, seeing the glory of the Lord as though reflected in a mirror, are being transformed into the same image from one degree of glory to another" (v. 18). According to Paul, we are transformed into the image of Jesus "from one degree of glory to another" by allowing the Spirit to use *our unveiled minds* to see Jesus's glory.

Paul reiterates the same point a few verses later when he notes that "the god of this world has blinded *the minds* of the unbelievers, to keep them from *seeing* the light of the gospel of the glory of Christ, who is the image of God" (4:4). By contrast, we who have unveiled minds are able to see "the light of the knowledge of the glory of God in the face of Jesus Christ" (4:6). The place where we "see" Jesus (or anything or anyone else) "in our mind" is *the imagination*. The imagination is just our word for the mind's ability to see images. So experiencing Jesus in our imagination is a biblical, not a "New Age," concept.

On top of this, the spiritual discipline of intentionally opening up one's imagination to experience Jesus has been practiced by disciples throughout Church history. This is sometimes referred to as the tradition of "Cataphatic Prayer," and within this tradition the imagination was sometimes referred to as "the inner sanctum" (the inner sacred place). Here is where we encounter Jesus in concrete, experiential, life-transforming ways. Clearly, there is nothing "New Age" about this concept.

Finally, one never finds counterfeit three-dollar bills, for there aren't any *legitimate* three-dollar bills. So what should we conclude about the Christian use of the imagination in light of the fact that *it is* often counterfeited?

Q2: How has the journey that led you to the cross-centered way of interpreting the OT's violence impacted your life?

A2: It removed every last vestige of concern I had that God might harbor a vengeful or even sinister side to him. It gave me permission to *completely* trust that God truly is as beautiful as he is revealed to be on Calvary. And it allowed me to embrace this complete trust while continuing to believe that the whole Bible, including its nastiest portraits of God, is "God-breathed." I am profoundly blessed to hear that it is having a similar impact on multitudes of others.

RECOMMENDED RESOURCES: Greg recommends the following material that is relevant to the material covered in this postscript.

Boyd, G. *Seeing Is Believing: Experiencing Jesus Through Imaginative Prayer.* Grand Rapids: Baker, 2004.

Boyd, I. P. *Imaginative Prayer: A Year Long Guide to Your Child's Spiritual Formation.* Downers Grove, IL: IVP, 2017.

Appendix 1: The Cruciform Hermeneutic in Summary

Cross Vision (CV) is a short summary overview of Greg's larger work *Crucifixion of the Warrior God: Interpreting the Old Testament's Violent Portraits of God in Light of The Cross (CWG)* in which Greg lays out his proposal for biblical interpretation called "the cruciform hermeneutic." In *CV* it's expressed as:

The Cornerstone	The Foundation of the *Cross Vision* Principles
The crucified Christ is the perfect revelation of God's love and the key to interpreting the violent passages of God in the Old Testament	1. The cross is the definitive revelation of God 2. All Scripture is breathed by God, so nothing can be dismissed. 3. Our understanding of God's "breathing" must be anchored in the cross. 4. All Scripture is interpreted through the lens of the cross 5. The cross reveals a God who will not coerce people into believing the truth.

In *CV*, the cruciform hermeneutic results in four cross-centered insights that help disclose how various violent portraits of God point to the cross. The chart below summarizes these insights and demonstrates how they are anchored in the cross.

The Heavenly Missionary and Divine Withdrawal	The Aikido Nature of God's Judgment	The Cosmic Conflict between God and the Powers of Darkness	The Misuse of Divinely Given Supernatural Power
In the OT, God is like a "heavenly missionary" who willingly accommodates the limited perspectives of God's people to maintain relationship with them until the full revelation of God in the crucified Christ takes place.	The judgment for sin is built into sin itself; God uses a form of "divine aikido," withdrawing God's protection to allow the self-destructive power of sin to run its course.	Much of the OT language about violence must be understood in the context of the cosmology of the ANE with its historically rooted understanding of "spiritual warfare."	When God endows individuals with supernatural power, he does not control how this power gets used. And some biblical characters misused divine power.
The death of Christ on the cross reveals God stooping to accommodate our sinfulness and taking on its ugly appearance, despite Jesus's beautiful innocence.	*The death of Christ on the cross reveals God withdrawing divine protection so sin and evil can run their full course and ultimately self-destruct.*	*The death of Christ on the cross reveals God conquering the cosmic powers and doing so in a way that God's cosmic enemies did not anticipate.*	*The death of Jesus on the cross only came about because Jesus fully submitted the use of his God-given supernatural authority to the Father's will.*

In *CWG*, the basic content is the same as the above, but the categories are presented as four specific cross-based principles (see diagram below): (1) *The Principle of Cruciform Accommodation*, (2) *The Principle of Redemptive Withdrawal*, (3) *The Principle of Cosmic Conflict*, and (4) *The Principle of Semiautonomous Power*.

Readers of *CV* who are looking for a broader, more academic discussion of each of these principles are encouraged to walk through *CWG*. I promise you, the challenge of engaging with that material is well worth the effort!

Appendix 2: Truth Priorities

When considering the cruciform hermeneutic, it's important to understand how much significance to give this type of approach. At Greg's church (Woodland Hills) their teaching team uses the diagram below to help determine what level of priority (i.e., how much "weight") to give various perspectives and ideas.

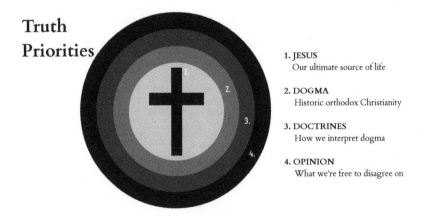

Truth Priorities

1. JESUS
   Our ultimate source of life

2. DOGMA
   Historic orthodox Christianity

3. DOCTRINES
   How we interpret dogma

4. OPINION
   What we're free to disagree on

The center of this "truth priorities" diagram is **the crucified Christ**. Greg encourages believers to anchor their ultimate well-being—that is, their innermost need to feel worthwhile, significant, and secure—in the crucified Christ. Greg refers to this core need as the hunger for "LIFE." So long as we rely on Christ alone for our LIFE, we could be mistaken about all our other beliefs, and it would not fundamentally alter our core well-being. Conversely, if we're not relying on Christ to meet this core need, we will be tempted to get LIFE from the rightness of a multitude of other things we believe. This is religious idolatry, and it explains why so many people feel threatened when others challenge their beliefs.

The layer outside the crucified Christ contains the historic **dogmas** that have defined the historic orthodox church throughout history. These dogmas reflect what all Christians have in common regardless of what denominational tradition they come from and are largely (though not exclusively) summed up in the Apostles Creed and the Nicene Creed.

The next layer contains the various **doctrines** of the church, representing various *interpretations* of the dogmas and illustrating how followers of Jesus don't always see eye-to-eye on some of the specifics of our shared Christian faith. For example, all orthodox Christians affirm the dogma that God providentially rules the world, but they espouse different doctrines regarding what this entails. Some believe God's providence means that everything that happens is in accordance with God's will, while others hold that God allows the free choices of angels and humans to affect what comes to pass.

The outer-most layer consists of all other theological **opinions** that individuals or groups have espoused on a variety of topics but that haven't been made into a doctrine by any major Christian denomination. They illustrate the numerous ways people across the Christian spectrum have tried to wrestle with specific Scriptures and concepts, how to understand those ideas, and how to apply them to the Christian life. These are things that faithful Christians should feel free to disagree on and should never divide over.

When it comes to the cruciform hermeneutic, Greg specifically puts this method of interpretation in the category of "**opinion**." As he has said, "This is my way of wrestling with a very difficult issue. There is no denomination that is formed on this approach, and we aren't going to start one. I am offering this to people who are struggling with the violent passages of God in the OT. If it works for you, wonderful! If not, find something better and let me know about it!"